Nature and Grace

# Nature and Grace

and other essays

## Karl Rahner

Professor of Dogmatic Theology
at the University of Innsbruck

Translated by Dinah Wharton

Sheed and Ward · London and Sydney

First published 1963
Sheed and Ward Ltd, 33 Maiden Lane, London WC2 and
Sheed and Ward Pty Ltd, 95 York Street, Sydney

Third impression 1968

Originally published as "Natur und Gnade", in the work
*Fragen der Theologie heute,* Verlagsanstalt Benziger & Co.,
Einsiedeln, and *Gefahren im heutigen Katholizismus,*
Johannes-Verlag, Einsiedeln.

Nihil obstat : Joannes M. T. Barton, STD, LSS,
   Censor Deputatus
Imprimatur : + Georgius L. Craven, Epūs Sebastopolis Vic. Cap.
Westmonasterii, die 31a Jan. 1963

*The* Nihil obstat *and* Imprimatur *are a declaration that a
book or pamphlet is considered to be free from doctrinal or
moral error. It is not implied that those who have granted
the* Nihil obstat *and* Imprimatur *agree with the contents,
opinions or statements expressed.*

Standard book number : 7220 0096 0

This book is set in 11 pt. Linotype Times
Made and printed in Great Britain by
William Clowes and Sons Ltd, London and Beccles

# CONTENTS

vi CONTENTS

# ABBREVIATIONS

| | |
|---|---|
| *DB* | Denzinger-Bannwart, *Enchiridion Symbolorum* |
| *GM* | *Gregorianum* |
| *NRT* | *Nouvelle revue théologique* |
| *RSPT* | *Revue des sciences philosophiques et théologiques* |
| *RSR* | *Recherches de science religieuse* |
| *RT* | *Revue thomiste* |
| *TS* | *Theological Studies* |
| *ZKT* | *Zeitschrift für katholische theologie* |

# PART 1

# NATURE AND GRACE

# 1

## NATURE AND GRACE[1]

B Y and large nowadays only "specialist circles" concern themselves with the subject "nature and grace". But at least it *is* again being talked about, and not disregarded except when mention of it cannot be avoided. It is a subject which arouses passionate discussion. Views differ over it and the controversy is not merely academic. This is splendid. For since the controversy between Catholic and Protestant theology died down and became sterile in the eighteenth century, and the traditional scholastic theology was won back in victory over the thin-blooded theology of the Enlightenment in the nineteenth century, for a short time it was generally thought that the subject "nature and grace" was closed, that everyone was agreed about it and more or less everything worth knowing was now known.

If we are going to try and describe this standard view of nature and grace in post-Tridentine and neo-scholastic theology, we must emphasize that

[1] It goes without saying that the bibliographical references given here can only represent a very limited and inevitably arbitrary selection of the dogmatic and historical literature on grace. And in general it will have to be confined to the last two centuries.

we really do mean *standard*. Of course the theology of today possesses all the riches of yesterday and all past ages. In the Church nothing is ever completely forgotten. And the truth expressly stated contains within it, unexpressed, depth upon depth of implications. And so it is easy to make mistakes in a description of the standard view of a subject in current theology. And yet this standard view does exist. And it is often more important in the Church's life than the sublimer insights of the few.

What was neo-scholasticism's standard view of the relationship between grace and nature? In order to see it as it really was (although it did not fully realize this itself), we must start from a problem in the doctrine of grace which is apparently only a peripheral problem. The supernatural grace through which man is justified and can do just works was regarded as something in itself beyond consciousness. This is a theological opinion, which has always been in dispute. For Thomist theology always held that a supernatural act has a formal object which can never be attained by a purely natural act. But the contrary opinion was the prevalent one and determined the standard view of the subject: Supernatural grace is a reality which we know about from the teaching of the Faith, but which is completely outside our experience and can never make its presence felt in our conscious personal life. We must strive for it,

knowing as we do through faith that it exists, take
care (through good moral acts and reception of
the sacraments) that we possess it, and treasure it
as our share in the divine life and the pledge and
necessary condition for life in heaven. But the
conscious sphere in which we experience ourselves
is not itself filled by this grace. We cannot experience what difference being supernaturally
"elevated" has made to our spiritual and moral
acts (the acts themselves as opposed to the objects,
distinct from the acts, which they are intentionally
directed towards). Thus, in this most widespread
view of it, grace is a superstructure above man's
conscious spiritual and moral life, although it is,
of course, also an acknowledged object of his faith
and recognized as the highest, the divine, life in
him which alone has power to bring him salvation.
It looks as if this conception must be the right one;
we can know nothing about our supernatural state
(or only conclude something about it with some
degree of probability from certain indications), we
cannot "see" anything of the action of grace (or at
most only those helps of "healing grace", which
are in themselves natural, to fulfil the natural
law). The simplest experience and the teaching of
the Council of Trent[1] (*DB*, 802, 805, 825, 826)

[1] On this teaching cf. A. Stakemeier, *Das Konzil von
Trient über die Heilsgewissheit*, Heidelberg, 1947; V.
Heynck, "Das Votum des Generals der Konventualen
Bonaventura Costacciaro vom 26. Nov. 1546 über die

seem to endorse this view almost as a matter of course. Once one has this view, then of course the sphere of our spiritual and moral actions, within which we are present to ourselves, seems to be identical with "nature" in the theological sense. And this sphere is even made a definition of what we mean by nature; nature is what we experience of ourselves without revelation, for this is nature and nature *only*. And vice versa, only nature and its acts constitute that life which we experience as ours. We make up from the elements of our natural powers, habits etc., those acts in which we intentionally direct ourselves towards God's revealed mysteries and which we know to be "essentially" (but only "essentially") supernaturally raised. Supernatural "enlightenment", moral "impulsion" and "inspiration" to do good,

---

Gnadengewissheit", *Franz Stud.* 31 (1949), pp. 274–304, 350–95; Fr. Buuck, "Zum Rechtfertigungsdekret. Die Unterscheidung zwischen fehlbarem und unfehlbarem Glauben in den vorbereitenden Verhandlungen"; Fr. J. Schierse, "Das Trienter Konzil und die Frage nach der christlichen Gewissheit": both in Georg Schreiber, *Das Weltkonzil von Trient*, Freiburg, 1951, Vol. 1, pp. 117–167; G. M. Lachance, "L'Homme peut-il savoir qu'il a la grâce?" *Rev. Univ. Ottawa*, 24 (1954), pp. 65–92; M. Guérard des Lauriers, "St. Augustin et la question de la certitude de la grâce au Concile de Trente" in *Augustinus Magister* (Congrès International Aug. 1954), Communications vol. 2, pp. 1057–67; L. M. Poliseno, "I Carmelitani e la certezza dello stato di grazia nel Concilio Tridentino", *Carmelus*, I (1954), pp. 111–45.

the "light" of faith, the working of the Holy Spirit
—scriptural and traditional terms like these are
reduced to this purely entitative elevation of our
natural moral acts, or to natural psychological
influences (which are, however, regarded as being,
under God's providence, directed towards our
supernatural salvation). In short, the relationship
between nature and grace is thought of as two
layers laid very carefully one on top of the other
so that they interpenetrate as little as possible.
And accordingly, nature's orientation towards
grace is thought of as negatively as possible. Indeed, grace is in fact the most perfect fulfilment of
nature; indeed, God the Lord of this nature can
require man to submit himself to his will that man
should have a supernatural life and destiny, and
to open himself to grace; but nature in itself has
only a *potentia obedientialis* to do this, thought of
as negatively as possible; the mere absence of a
contradiction in such an elevation of nature.
Nature itself can be fulfilled in a purely natural
destiny, content and harmonious in its own sphere,
without direct contact with God in the Beatific
Vision; when it turns in on itself in its immediate
self-awareness (as it is in the nature of spirit to do:
*reditio completa in seipsum*) it is aware of itself as
if it were a "pure nature". In its present fallen
state it differs from "pure nature" only, in the
words of the well-known phrase (which is an
opinion, not a definition), *sicut spoliatus a nudo—*

as the man who has lost his clothes differs from the man who has never had any. The lack of grace is only thought of as a deprivation because of a decree of God (which "demands the possession of grace") and an event in the past (Adam's sin); it is not as if the lack itself were any different in the two cases.

This standard view cannot be acquitted of a certain "extrinsicity", as it has been called— granted, of course, that when formulated with proper precision it can be shown not to go against any teaching of the magisterium on the relationship between nature and grace. Neither can we deny (although we sometimes may not like hearing this said) that in practice it is not without danger. For if it is the true view, then all that man can experience of his spiritual life takes place within the bounds of nature alone, and this nature is divided into two sectors: the "purely natural", which (with its supernatural elevation considered as completely above consciousness) is the life of nature alone, and then those acts (e.g., faith or the desire to serve God) which are (subjectively) constituted of purely natural elements and are only directed towards the supernatural as their object. If this is so, then it is not surprising (although of course not always justified) when a man takes very little interest in this mysterious superstructure of his being; this grace is not present where he is present to himself, in his immediate self-awareness. One can get the impression (although it may not be objectively justified) that during the course of the theological development in the Middle Ages, what had originally been called grace came to be thought of as the act of nature performed with natural powers (e.g., the power to love God above all things), and in order to get round this, what was basically the same thing was superimposed upon nature and called "supernature", and then, of course, it was pushed away into the region above the consciousness and became an unconscious modality of the spiritual and moral in nature, and it was hard to see what further use it could be. Think, for example, of the distinction—right, of course, in a certain sense—between natural and supernatural "love of God above all things"; how can these two loves differ *as love*, i.e., spiritual, when the supernaturalness of the supernatural love only rests in an entitative "elevation"? Would one be completely mistaken in seeing a connection with modern naturalism of this theory too? If it is true that the modern lack of interest in the supernatural could only have developed on the basis of this conception of grace (which is of course in some measure nominalistic)?

Theological controversy has again become strong over the question of the correctness or adequacy of this conception. There are several reasons for this.

*Philosophically* the kind of scholastic philosophy connected with the work of J. Maréchal[1] was involved. In his intellectual, transcendental dynamism, Maréchal sees man (in so far as he is spirit, thus in his "nature") as in his very essence "desiderium naturale visionis beatificae" (to give him St. Thomas's phrase). This desire is, of course, conditional and so it does not take away the freedom of his actual vocation to the direct vision of God through grace, and it is fundamentally present in every spiritual act in the form of a longing for the absolute Being (without therefore being explicitly and conceptually formulated). It is the *a priori* condition of every affirmation and acceptance of any finite thing. In this recourse to the doctrine of a natural desire for the direct vision of God we can see already how from a minor corollary (or so it seems) in St. Thomas, it became for Maréchal the key to the understanding of a spiritual nature. It is understandable that in the thirties there was a long debate over the meaning attached by Maréchal and his school to this natural desire, and whether it could be squared with the Church's teaching that the direct vision

---

[1] In this short theological essay no bibliography will be given of this philosophical trend which was of great importance in the meeting of scholastic and modern philosophy. Many Catholic philosophers of today are indebted to a greater or lesser extent to the teaching of Maréchal, e.g., Hayen, A. Grégoire, Siewerth, Max Müller, K. Lotz and many others.

of God is supernatural and gratuitous.[1] At any rate, it began to be understood that the orientation of man as a spirit towards God is not an "extra", but it is what makes him what he experiences himself to be and he cannot finally deny and repress it without sin, because it is affirmed (even if only as an implicit, transcendental *a priori*) in every act of his spirit.

In the field of history of theology[2] the main

[1] Cf., for example, E. Brisbois, "Désir naturel et vision de Dieu", NRT, 54 (1927), pp. 81–97; H. Lennerz, "Kann die Vernunft die Möglichkeit der beseligenden Anschauung Gottes beweisen?", *Schol.*, 5 (1930), pp. 102–8; H. Lennerz, "Ist die Anschauung Gottes ein Geheimnis?", *Schol.*, 7 (1932), pp. 208–32; M. Corvez, "Est-il possible de démontrer l'existence en Dieu d'un ordre de mystères strictement surnaturels?", *RT*, 37 (1932), pp. 660–67; R. Garrigou-Lagrange, "La possibilité de la vision béatifique peut-elle se démontrer?", RT, 38 (1933), pp. 669–88; further literature in *Bull. Thom.*, 1932, pp. 745–69; 1935, pp. 896–907; *Bull. Thom.*, V (1937 ff.), pp. 632–43; 728; P. Descoqs, *Le Mystère de notre élévation surnaturelle*, Paris, 1938; further literature in Z. Alszeghy, *Greg.*, 31 (1950), pp. 444–6. Bound up with this whole problem is the question whether or not this orientation towards God held by Maréchal can demonstrate at the least the possibility of the Beatific Vision. We cannot go into it here.

[2] Only a small selection of the literature of the last twenty-five years can be given here. Biblical theology will be omitted, because on the whole it has, unfortunately, had little influence on the dogmatic theology of the schools during this period. First must be mentioned the survey of the whole history of the theology of grace

by H. Rondet, then a few works on patrology, then
medieval and modern history of the theology of grace:
H. Rondet, *Gratia Christi. Essai d'histoire du dogme et
de théologie dogmatique*, Paris, 1948; H. Rahner, "Die
Gottesgeburt. Die Lehre der Kirchenväter von der
Geburt Christi im Herzen der Gläubigen", *ZKT*, 59
(1935), pp. 333–418; E. Mersch, *Le Corps mystique du
Christ*, Louvain, 1936, 1–2; A. Lieske, *Die Theologie
der Logomystik bei Origenes*, Münster, 1938; J. Gross,
*La Divinisation du chrétien d'après les pères grecs*,
Paris, 1938; A. Lieske, "Zur Theologie der Christus-
mystik Gregors von Nyssa", *Schol.*, 14 (1939), pp. 408–
514; J. Loosen, *Logos und Pneuma im begnadeten
Menschen bei Maximus Confessor*, Münster, 1941; A.
Mayer, *Das Bild Gottes im Menschen nach Clemens
von Alexandrien*, Rome, 1942; H. Urs von Balthasar,
*Présence et pensée. Essai sur la philosophie religieuse de
Grégoire de Nysse*, Paris, 1942; J. B. Schoemann,
"Gregors von Nyssa theologische Anthropologie als
Bildtheologie", *Schol.*, 18 (1943), pp. 31–53, 175–200;
J. Daniélou, *Platonisme et théologie mystique. Essai
sur la doctrine spirituelle de saint Grégoire de Nysse*,
Paris, 1944; H. du Manoir, *Dogme et spiritualité chez
saint Cyrille d'Alexandrie*, Paris, 1945; P. Galtier, *Le
Saint-Esprit en nous d'après les pères grecs*, Rome, 1946;
A. Lieske, "Die Theologie der Christusmystik Gregors
von Nyssa", *ZKT*, 70 (1948), pp. 49–93, 129–68, 315–40;
J. Grabowski, "St. Augustine and the Presence of God",
*TS*, 13 (1952), pp. 336–48; E. Braem, "Augustinus' leer
over de heiligmakende genade", *Augustiniana*, I (1951),
pp. 7–20, 77–90; II (1952), pp. 201–4; III (1953), pp. 328–
340; IV (1954), pp. 196–204; H. Merki, *Homoiosis Theo.
Von der platonischen Angleichung an Gott sur Gottähn-
lichkeit bei Gregor von Nyssa*, Freiburg, Switzerland,
1952; H. Doms, *Die Gnadenlehre des seligen Albertus
Magnus*, Breslau, 1929; J. Schupp, *Die Gnadenlehre des
Petrus Lombardus*, Freiburg, 1932; F. Stegmüller, *Zur*

concern was with the history of theological reflex
knowledge of the supernatural, and how it differs
from the natural. It was realized that the modern
theological concept of the supernatural (and the

---

Gnadenlehre des jungen Suarez, Freiburg, 1933; F.
Stegmüller, Francisco de Vitoria y la doctrina de la
gracia en la escuela salmantina, Barcelona, 1934; F.
Stegmüller, Geschichte des Molinismus I: Neue Molina-
schriften, Münster, 1935; E. Köster, Die Heilslehre des
Hugo von St. Viktor, Emsdetten, 1940; H. Bouillard,
Conversion et grâce chez saint Thomas d'Aquin, Paris,
1944; R. C. Dhont, Le Problème de la préparation à la
grâce. Débuts de l'école franciscaine, Paris, 1946; M.
Flick, L'Attimo della giustificazione secondo S.
Tommaso, Rome, 1947; Z. Alszeghy, "La teologia
dell'ordine soprannaturale nella scolastica antica",
Greg., 31 (1950), pp. 414–50 (survey of recent literature);
S. Gonzalez Rivas, "Suarez frente al misterio de la
inhabitacion", Estud. Ecl., 24 (1950), pp. 341–66; J. Auer,
Entwicklung der Gnadenlehre in der Hochscholastik mit
besonderer Berücksichtigung des Kardinals Matteo d'
Aquasparta I, Freiburg, 1942, II, Freiburg, 1951;
A. M. Landgraf, Dogmengeschichte der Frühscholastik,
Part I, vols. 1–2: Die Gnadenlehre Regensburg, 1951–
1952; H. Lais, Die Gnadenlehre des hl. Thomas in der
Summa contra Gentiles und der Kommentar des
Franziskus Sylvestris von Ferrara, Münich, 1951; J.
Alfaro, Lo natural y lo sobrenatural. Estudio historico
desde santo Thomas hasta Cayetano (1274–1534),
Madrid, 1952; O. Lottin, Psychologie et morale aux XIIe
et XIIIe siècles, Louvain, 1942–54, I, II, III, 1–2, IV,
1–2; W. A. van Roo, Grace and Original Justice according to St. Thomas, Rome, 1955; Z. Alszeghy, Nova
creatura. La nozione della grazia nei commentari
medievali di S, Paolo, Rome, 1956.

natural as its counterpart) only developed slowly
and the application of these terms to the many
individual theological problems was only slowly
worked out (problems, for example, like the
necessity of strictly supernatural and internal
grace for every act profitable to salvation; the
possibility of distinguishing between natural and
supernatural morality and defining the boundaries
between them; the difference between supernatural
actual and habitual grace; the impossibility of
positive preparation for justification through
moral acts performed without saving grace;
whether a purely natural destiny for man after
death is conceivable). On the whole it is true to
say that the development has been legitimate and
a true unfolding of the facts given in revelation;
it has not been a false development. It is also true
that with St. Thomas it had already progressed
far enough to make what comes later clearly
visible in him (which is not to say that he reached
the point reached by Cajetan and post-Tridentine
theology). But now we are getting a picture of the
process of development itself. We see more clearly
that we cannot read all the later insights and distinctions into the earlier theology. And because
we can see this we are in a better position to
inquire whether during the process of development earlier valuable knowledge has not been
lost, whether the gain has not been at the cost of
the loss of other knowledge, and that there is,

therefore, much to be regained which theology once possessed. It may be that there is a tendency to overrate the difference between medieval (especially St. Thomas's) and post-Tridentine theology of grace. It may be that in the grace theology of the seventeenth- and eighteenth-century "Augustinians" there are elements which should not be considered tenable today simply because Benedict XIV declared them free of hidden Jansenism. When we realize the special nature of the history of thought on a subject, and when we realize that it cannot simply be divided up into the history of thought on the clear unchanging truth never disputed by really orthodox theologians, and the history of wicked heretical teachings, our historical study not only shows us how we arrived at the final form of modern theology, but enables us to rediscover the intentions and preoccupations of earlier theologians which have been forgotten in modern textbook theology, always in danger, as it is, of making the manageable and simplified the criterion of the truth and of hallowed tradition. We discover (to give just a few examples from our own subject) that the concept of the "natural desire for the Beatific Vision" in St. Thomas is not merely a left-over, to be explained "historically" from the time when theology was not yet so explicit about the supernatural and gratuitous nature of the direct vision of God (which, of course, it *is* in this case); that behind the hesitation to postulate a strictly supernatural actual grace (as well as habitual) lies not *only* a faulty terminology only slowly to be put right, which does not grasp that the saving acts, which are done before justification and yet cannot be done without grace, necessarily require the existence of actual grace[1]; that we can learn something today from St. Thomas about the relationship between sacrament and personal act which was forgotten or simplified in later theology; that medieval theology thought much more deeply about "uncreated grace" than post-Tridentine official theology, which thought of the "indwelling of the Spirit of God" more or less exclusively in terms of "created grace", and in its anti-Protestant zeal was too ready to call created grace simply "grace".

A third incentive to reapproach the question of the relationship between nature and grace has come from the revival of the dialogue between Catholic and Protestant theology.[2] In the nature

[1] St. Thomas considered the actual acts of "preparation" for justification as acts of justification "taking over", done with the grace of justification already present; and so he did not need to concern himself very much with the acts of preparation which precede justification in time; he has thus something new to tell *us*, not only we him.

[2] Out of the Catholic works we will mention here only the following: H. Urs von Balthasar, "Deux Notes sur Karl Barth", *RSR*, 35 (1948), pp. 92–111; J. Hamer, *Karl*

of the case Protestant theologians are bound to be concerned with this problem too (although, of course, from different points of view). And they have recently re-examined it, taking as their starting-point the Bible, Luther, and controversy with modern humanism and Anglo-Saxon-American optimism. They were bound to ask what else is man besides a sinner, how far does he remain a sinner when he has been justified. We find in early Protestant doctrine that in man without grace there is absolutely nothing good (which serves towards *salvation*). But this teaching (which, rightly understood, is held also by Catholics) is only the beginning of the investigation; and this is where there are new possibilities of discussion with Catholic theologians. And these opportunities have already been partially made use of. And, vice versa, Catholic theology has been driven to examine afresh (even though only a few Catholic theologians may actually be doing so) what is right in the Protestant doctrine and how it can be made more clearly valid for us; we must

Barth. *L'occasionalisme théologique de Karl Barth. Étude sur la méthode dogmatique*, Paris, 1949; H. Volk, *Emil Brunners Lehre von dem Sünder*, Münster, 1950; H. Urs von Balthasar, *Karl Barth. Darstellung und Deutung seiner Theologie*, Cologne, 1951; A. Ebneter, *Der Mensch in der Theologie Karl Barths*, Zürich, 1952; H. Küng, *Rechtfertigung. Die Lehre Karl Barths und eine katholische Besinnung*, Einsiedeln, 1957.

see Christ as the centre of the whole existing world and economy of salvation; we must show that the supernaturalness of grace does not mean that man in his "natural" being is a closed system complete in itself with grace as a pure superstructure which leaves what is beneath unchanged; we must investigate whether and in what sense a Catholic can hold the axiom "simul justus et peccator"; we must make our own the idea of existential, personal "moments of grace", which is also implicit in and proper to the Catholic doctrine of grace, and we must clear up the misunderstanding which leads people to think that the idea of a "state" of grace, when grace is "present" but not necessarily "active", is an aberration from the true biblical doctrine of grace.

We need not waste much time in saying that the "modern mentality" has stimulated theological thought in this direction. We want a single complete picture of man, we want a synthesis of all the different things we know about him. We think "existentially". And so we want as far as possible to "experience" the reality of grace in our own existence where we experience ourselves; we want to see and feel its power at work in us. And in accordance with other modern tendencies, we shall not only want to see grace as it concerns the individual, but also consider more explicitly its ecclesiological aspects, grace in the history of salvation not only within the Church, the possibility of grace and its highest manifestations in the world of non-Christian religions.

When in what follows we give the "findings" of these theological investigations, of course this does not mean that they have already been officially accepted or already become *sententia communis*. The development of the Church's teaching does not progress so quickly. Especially when, as at the moment, immediate problems of the day (particularly moral problems) and Mariology demand even more attention than these more complex problems, which inevitably need a long time to ripen. And so here we can do no more than tentatively outline the main line of development of these investigations.

We may hold that the problem of "uncreated grace" can be carried further.[1] Pius XII said in

[1] We mention only the most recent works on all the problems connected with the question of uncreated grace and appropriated or unappropriated indwelling of the divine persons: H. Kuhaupt, *Die Formalursache der Gotteskindschaft*, Münster, 1940; H. Schauf, *Die Einwohnung des Heiligen Geistes. Die Lehre von der nichtappropriierten Einwohnung des Heiligen Geistes als Beitrag zur Theologiegeschichte des neunzehnten Jahrhunderts unter besonderer Berücksichtigung der beiden Theologen Carl Passaglia und Clemens Schrader*, Freiburg, 1941; "The Inhabitation of the Holy Spirit: A Solution According to De la Taille", *TS*, 8 (1947), pp. 445–70; J. Trütsch, *SS. Trinitatis inhabitatio apud theologos recentiores*, Trent, 1949; S. J. Dockx, *Fils de Dieu par grâce*, Paris, 1948; C. Sträter, "Het begrip

his encyclical *Mystici Corporis* that there are
questions here still open and purposely left open
by the Church's magisterium. If (as Pius XII says)
grace and glory are two stages of the one process
of divinization, and, as classical theology has
always held, in glory God communicates himself
to the supernaturally elevated created spirit in a
communication which is not the *efficient* causal
creation of a creaturely quality or entity distinct
from God, but the quasi-formal causal communication of God himself, then this can also be

'appropriatie' bij S. Thomas", *Bijdr.*, 9 (1948), pp. 1–41,
144–86; J. H. Nicolas, "Présence trinitaire et présence
de la Trinité", *RT*, 50 (1950), pp. 183–91; J. Fitzgerald,
*De Inhabitatione Spiritus Sancti Doctrina Sancti Thomae
Aquinatis*, Mundelein, 1950; R. Morency, *L'Union de
grâce selon saint Thomas d'Aquin*, Montreal, 1950; P.
Galtier, *L'habitation en nous des trois personnes*, Rome,
1950; H. P. C. Lyons, "The Grace of Sonship", *Eph. Th.
Lov.*, 27 (1951), pp. 438–66; C. Kaliba, *Die Welt als
Gleichnis des dreieinigen Gottes. Entwurf zu einer trini-
tarischen Ontologie*, Salzburg, 1952; P. de Letter,
"Sanctifying Grace and Our Union With the Holy
Trinity", *TS*, 13 (1952), pp. 35–58; P. J. Donnelly,
"Sanctifying Grace and Our Union with the Holy
Trinity: A Reply", *TS*, 13 (1952), pp. 190–204; F.
Bourassa, "Adoptive Sonship. Our Union with the
Divine Persons", *TS*, 13 (1952), pp. 309–35; P. de Letter,
"Current Theology. Sanctifying Grace and the Divine
Indwelling", *TS*, 14 (1953), pp. 242–72; F. Bourassa,
"Présence de Dieu et union aux divines personnes", *Sc.
Eccl.*, 6 (1954), pp. 3–23; K. Rahner, "Zur scholastischen
Begrifflichkeit der ungeschaffenen Gnade", in *Schriften
zur Theologie*, 1.

applied to *grace* much more explicitly than it commonly has been in theology up till now. "Uncreated grace" will then no longer be regarded as merely the consequence of the creation of "infused" grace, constituting the state of grace, as a "physical accident"; but rather as the very essence of grace (which also explains much better how grace can strictly be a mystery, for a purely created entity as such can never be an absolute mystery). God communicates himself to man in his own reality. That is the mystery and the fullness of grace. From this the bridge to the mystery of the Incarnation and the Trinity is easier to find.

The theory (already held by Petavius, Scheeben and others) seems to be gaining ground that in grace a relationship is established between man and each of the three divine persons which is not an appropriation but a *proprium* of each divine person. If the direct vision of God can only be founded on the quasi-formal causal self-communication of God and not (adequately) on a created quality in the spirit of man, and if (as is self-evident) the three divine persons are the object of this direct vision each *as* a single Person, then the essential (ontic) quasi-formal communication of God, which replaces the *species impressa* as the ontological ground of man's knowing possession of God, must also imply a non-appropriated relationship of each of the three divine persons to man. And thence the relationship between the

"immanent" Trinity and the Trinity in the
economy of salvation could be rethought, and
the highest mystery of the Christian faith be seen
more clearly as a reality with which man has to
do not only intellectually (and through the incarnation of the Word), but also actually in the
living of his life of grace. It would be realized
that God is not only tri-personal in himself, but
also communicates himself tri-personally (in grace
which is not only an external efficient causality of
God as *creatio ex nihilo*), although, of course, it
always remains true that wherever God exercises
his *efficient* causality this is always the work of
the whole Trinity as one single cause.

Perhaps we should go even further. The connection between the Incarnation and the order of
grace is usually regarded as purely factual.[1] In fact
God willed that the order of grace should be de-
pendent on the incarnate Word. It is tacitly pre-
supposed that it could have been otherwise. Is this
presupposition clearly and certainly right? The
order of grace and the Incarnation both depend
on a free gift of God. But does it follow that
these two objects of his free gift, in both of

[1] Cf. N. Sanders, "Een bovennatuurlijke orde mogelijk
zonder Christus?", *Stud. Cath.*, 29 (1954), pp. 152–8;
K. Rahner, "Zur Theologie der Weihnachtsfeier",
*Schriften zur Theologie*, III (Einsiedeln, 1956), pp. 35–
46; K. Rahner, "Die ewige Bedeutung der Menschheit
Jesu für unser Gottesverhältnis", *Schriften zur Theologie*,
III (Einsiedeln, 1956), pp. 47–60.

which he communicates his very self to man
(although of course in different ways), are two
acts of his loving freedom? Isn't it possible (on
Catholic principles) to hold with the Scotists that
the original act of God (which settles everything
else) is his emptying of himself, Love giving up
himself, in the Incarnation, so that with the
Incarnation the order of grace is already there
and without this decision of God to give up himself it would be quite inconceivable? And who
can produce fully convincing arguments to refute
the man who holds that the *possibility* of the
Creation depends on the possibility of the Incarnation, which is not to say that the reality of the
Creation (as nature) necessarily involves that the
Incarnation should happen. If this is accepted (its
very simplicity recommends it even apart from
other more positive indications, e.g., pre-Nicene
and pre-Augustinian Logos-theology), then grace
takes on a much more radically christological
character; the incarnate Word come into the
world is not only the actual mediator of grace
through his merit (which is only necessary because
Adam lost this grace), but by his free coming into
the world he makes the world's order of nature
his nature, which presupposes him, and the
world's order of grace his grace and his *milieu*.
And from this point, as we said, it would be
possible to reach a much deeper understanding of
the inner life of the Trinity. The Word would not

then be only one of the divine persons any of
whom could become man if he wanted to, but *the*
person in whom God communicates himself hypo-
statically to the world; the Incarnation mirrors the
unique personal character of the second divine
person, the Word. From the Trinity's external
work we can get a glimpse into their inner life.
This cannot be impossible because the axiom that
the efficient causality of God in his external acts
is a causality of the three persons acting together
as the one God cannot be applied to quasi-formal
causality. At this point the speculation of pre-
Nicene and Greek theology needs to be re-
examined. It will appear that in this Augustine
understood too little of the earlier theology, that
precisely the Logos is the one who appears and
must appear if God wants to show himself per-
sonally to the world.

From a more precise understanding of "uncreated grace" we can also see more clearly that
because of the very thing which distinguishes the
Catholic theology of grace (that grace is not only
pardon for the poor sinner but "sharing in the
divine nature"), the idea that it holds grace to be
merely a created state in the order of being, and
so merely "ontic" and unexistential—a "physical
accident"—cannot be maintained.[1] Grace is God
himself, his communication, in which he gives

[1] J. Auer, "Um den Begriff der Gnade", *ZKT*, 70
(1948), pp. 341–68.

himself to us as the divinizing loving kindness
which is himself. Here his work is really *himself*,
as the one communicated. From the very first this
grace cannot be conceived as separable from
God's personal love and man's answer to it. This
grace must not be thought of "materialistically";
it is only put "at man's disposal" by letting itself
be used as is the way with the freest grace of all,
the miracle of love. We only think here in ontic
categories (also Catholic) because a Catholic
theology has got to think of the real (and what
more real and more powerful than the love of
God?) as "real" and "existing", has got to express
the highest things in the most abstract words, and
so God's act of love to us, precisely because it is
God's and not our act (although of course it frees
us not only to have things done to us but to do
things), must be thought of as coming before our
act of love and faith and making this act possible,
and thus, inevitably, it must be thought of in
categories of being—state, accident, habit, in-
fusion etc. These expressions do not lead anyone
astray who understands them and never forgets
that grace is always the free act of God's love
which man can "dispose" of *only* in the measure
in which he himself is at this love's disposal. We
must of course always remember that God does
not thereby become smaller but man greater. And
finally we must realize that Christianity is not a
religion based only on the feelings; our praise of

2

the greatness to which God has raised us, and thus our praise of God, must come from our minds too, and not only our grateful hearts. This is true of Mariology and it is true of the doctrine of grace, of which Mariology is only the most beautiful part.

Grace also penetrates our conscious life, not only our essence but our existence too. The teaching of St. Thomas[1] on the specific object of the entitatively supernaturally elevated act, an object which (*qua* formal) cannot be reached by any natural act, must be rethought and made prevalent again. Here "object" does not mean "objectively given, distinguishable from others through reflection and seen together *with* others". A formal object is neither an object of knowledge nor just the bringing together of what is common

[1] This is not the place to quote the textbooks which deal with this question. Let us only note in passing that it is also of great importance for the problem of the foundation of faith. Cf. A. Lang, *Die Wege der Glaubensbegründung bei den Theologen des 14. Jahrhunderts*, Münster, 1930; F. Schlagenhaufen, "Die Glaubensgewissheit und ihre Begründung in der Neuscholastik", *ZKT*, 56 (1932), pp. 313–74, 530–95; G. Engelhardt, *Die Entwicklung der dogmatischen Glaubenspsychologie in der mittelalterlichen Scholastik vom Abälardsstreit bis zu Philip dem Kanzler*, Münster, 1933; R. Aubert, *Le Problème de l'acte de foi*, 2nd edition, Louvain, 1950; Cf. also K. Rahner, "Über die Erfahrung der Gnade", *Schriften zur Theolgie*, III (Einsiedeln, 1956), pp. 105–9.

to many individual objects by abstracting it afterwards; it is the *a-priori* "mental horizon", which we are conscious of in being conscious of ourselves, which is the context for all our knowing and recognizing of *a-posteriori* individual objects. If we take the ancient scholastic teaching of the formal object as the "light" by which and in which all other objects are seen, then we can't object to the Thomist doctrine of the supernatural formal object on the grounds that it cannot be "experienced". We must, moreover, remember that the *a-priori* formal object of an act is conceptually different from another formal object clearly distinguishable from it on reflection afterwards. There is no particular difficulty for a metaphysic of knowledge in seeing that transcendence to being at all, the natural openness to being as a whole, is not clearly distinguishable in reflection afterwards from the supernatural transcendence, by grace, of the Spirit, in every one of its supernaturally elevated acts, to the God of eternal life and to the immediate experience of (threefold) Being, although both kinds of transcendence (formal object of the natural spirit and formal object of the supernaturally elevated spirit) are conscious. From these very brief considerations on the metaphysics of the spirit we can see St. Thomas's doctrine to be fully defensible. And it recommends itself further by being the metaphysical-theological translation of the conviction expressed in Scripture. For if one honestly and unprejudicedly reads Scripture as it is and does not correct it by tacitly assuming that it can't be saying this because it is "wrong", then one has to admit that Scripture does not think of the gift of the Spirit (the divine *pneuma*) as only an entitative "elevation" above man's consciousness of his acts, which in his consciousness and existentially remain the same and are only changed through the Faith which comes from hearing; it is rather "life", "anointing", "comfort", "light", "interceding for us with unutterable groaning", *pneuma*, which is more than *nous*, inner impulsion, witness of the Spirit etc. It would be good if the teaching of Scripture was confronted point by point with this scholastic controversy. Then we should be rid once and for all of the tacit assumption that in a serious and weighty religious question we can take it for granted *a priori* that we shall get no more clear help from Scripture if the question is being debated among theologians, because if this were the case it would have been decided long ago. If all theological opinions were to recognize that supernatural actual graces are to be qualified as "enlightenments" and "inspirations", then this teaching of tradition would have to be taken seriously. It could not have an anti-Thomist interpretation put on it which would take away all its meaning. For an entitatively elevated act, which on the conscious level remains a natural act, cannot (without making the words meaningless) be called an inner enlightenment and inspiration. The very fact that the anti-Thomist—i.e., Molinist—thesis seeks to keep these words and find a meaning for them shows how strong is the conviction of tradition that the supernatural act performed through grace is also different spiritually, i.e., consciously and existentially and not only entitatively, from every natural act.

At this point we can note, and should be able to see more clearly than usual, that not only the justified perform supernatural acts. There are impulsions by grace which precede the acceptance of justification in free faith and love. And there is grace outside the Church and her sacraments. If we think of God's invitation by grace to the man compelled towards the possibility of making an existential decision in his immediate spiritual development not as intermittent grace, "actual" in the sense that it is temporary and is only given in special circumstances (and there is no theological reason which forces us to do so), but mean by "actual" only that the grace is specially given for an existential decision, as an "invitation" and as a "possibility" (to act freely for salvation), if we consider that in this sense man's moral freedom is not curtailed but continues to be at his disposal even when he has been given by grace the possibility of performing supernatural acts,[1] then we can say that this supernatural transcendence exists in every man who has reached the use of reason. He is not necessarily thereby justified, he can be a sinner and an unbeliever; but in so far as he has the concrete possibility of doing morally good actions he is open to transcendence to the God of supernatural life, whether his free action accords with or contradicts this potentiality of his supernaturally elevated spiritual existence. *If* in each moral act he takes up a positive or negative position towards the *totality* of his actual existence (and this we do not need to go into here), then we should have to say that every morally good act done by a man is in the order of salvation also a supernatural act of salvation. Then we should have come to the well-known opinion of Ripalda. This need not dismay us. For in the first place, although Ripalda's thesis has not often been advocated, it has never been forbidden; and in the second place, we could give up the supposition (that we do take up a positive or negative position in each moral act) which leads us to Ripalda's conclusion, without having to give up our basic position. We have shown this by the line of argument which we have outlined; it is perfectly

[1] The necessary condition of being able to believe at all. In Straub's theory everyone who has reached the use of reason can have this as "fides stricte dicta sed virtualis".

acceptable to hold that man's whole spiritual life is permanently penetrated by grace. Just because grace is *free and unmerited* this does not mean that it is rare (theology has been led astray for too long already by the tacit assumption that grace would no longer be grace if God became too free with it). Our whole spiritual life takes place within God's will for our salvation, his prevenient grace, his call making itself heard; all this is going on, perhaps unrecognized (if it is not recognized from the message of Faith coming from outside), in our conscious sphere of existence. Man lives consciously even when he does not "know" it and does not believe it, i.e., cannot make it an individual object of his knowledge merely by introspection. This is the inexpressible but existing ground of the dynamic power of all spiritual and moral life in the actual sphere of spiritual existence founded by God, i.e., supernaturally elevated, a "merely *a-priori*" existing ground, but still existing, something which we are conscious of in being conscious of ourselves, not as an object, but nevertheless existing.

We do not need to explain that this supernatural *a priori* in our spiritual existence, even though it can only be clearly brought to light and turned into objective knowledge through interpretation by revelation coming from without, nevertheless manifests itself in a thousand ways as a secret entelechy of individual and collective life, which would not happen if it were not at work. It follows from this that the history of religion, even outside the official history of revelation, is not just the result of natural reason and sin but the result of natural spirit, grace and sin (also in its *conscious* history, in its objective spirit). When a man is called by the message of faith of the visible Church, this call does not come to a man who is brought by it (and by his conceptual knowledge) for the first time into contact with the reality proclaimed; but it is a call which makes him reflect on and realize (and of course makes him take up a position towards) what was before the unrealized but truly existing grace present in him as an element of his spiritual existence. Preaching is the awakening and making explicit of what is already there in the depths of man, not by nature but by grace. Grace which enfolds man, the sinner and the unbeliever too, as his very sphere of existence which he can never escape from.

At this point we have now at last reached and can properly formulate the actual problem[1]

[1] We can only give here a somewhat arbitrary selection of the literature about this controversy, which centres mainly on the historical and theological works of H. de Lubac. We then mention several articles on the teaching of the encyclical *Humani Generis*, for as is well known, this encyclical also took up a position on this question. Further articles on *Humani Generis* are listed in, e.g., *Revista Espagnola de Teologia*, 11 (1951), pp. 173–6, 311–39; H. de Lubac, "Remarques sur l'histoire du mot 'surnaturel'", *NRT*, 61 (1934), pp. 225–49, 350–70; J.

Martinez-Gomez, "Notas sobre unas notas para la historia de la palabra sobrenatural", *Arch. T. Gran.*, 1 (1938), pp. 57–85; H. de Lubac, *Surnaturel. Études historiques*, Paris, 1946; H. Rondet, "Nature et surnaturel dans la théologie de St. Thomas d'Aquin", *RSR*, 33 (1947), pp. 379–95; C. Boyer, "Nature pure et surnaturel dans le 'Surnaturel' du Père de Lubac", *Greg.*, 28 (1947), pp. 379–95; G. de Broglie, *De Fine Ultimo Humanae Vitae. Pars prior, positiva*, Paris, 1948; H. Rondet, "Le Problème de la nature pure et la théologie du XVI siècle", *RSR*, 36 (1949), pp. 80–121; P. J. Donelly, "The Gratuity of the Beatific Vision and the Possibility of a Natural Destiny", *TS*, 11 (1950), pp. 374–404 (bibliography); W. Brugger, "Das Ziel des Menschen und das Verlangen nach der Gotteschau", *Schol.*, 25 (1950), pp. 535–48; M. J. de Guillou, "Surnaturel", *RSPT*, 34 (1950), pp. 226–43; R. Paniker, *El concepto de naturaleza. Analisis historico y metafisico de un concepto*, Madrid, 1951; G. Wiegel, "Historical Background of the Encyclical *Humani Generis*", *TS*, 12 (1951), pp. 520–49; J. Simon, "Transcendance et immanence dans la doctrine de la grâce", *Rev. Univ. Ottawa*, 21 (1951), pp. 344–69; L. Renwart, "La 'Nature pure' à la lumière de l'encyclique *Humani Generis*", *NRT*, 74 (1952), pp. 337–54; E. Gutwenger, "Natur und Übernatur" *ZKT*, 75 (1953), pp. 82–97; H. Urs von Balthasar-Gutwenger, "Der Begriff der Natur in der Theologie", *ZKT*, 75 (1953), pp. 452–64; J. Ternus, "Natur-Übernatur in der vortridentinischen Theologie seit Thomas von Aquin", *Schol.*, 28 (1953), pp. 399–404; M. R. Gagnebet, "L'Enseignement du magistère et le problème du surnaturel", *RT*, 53 (1953), pp. 5–27; L. Malevez, "La Gratuité du surnaturel", *NRT*, 75 (1953), pp. 561–86; K. Rahner, "Über die Verhältnis von Natur und Gnade", *Schriften zur Theologie* I (Einsideln, 1954), pp. 323–45; R. Bruch, "Das Verhältnis von Natur und Gnade nach der Auffassung der neueren Theologie", *Th. Gl.*, 46 (1956), pp. 81–102.

"nature and grace" in the narrower sense. It is clear that in the living of his mental and spiritual life man is aware of his "nature", even in the theological sense in which it is the opposite to grace and the supernatural. For when he reflects on himself, he experiences himself in every judgement of himself in which he looks at himself as an object and sees himself in his transcendence towards the infinite as something which he is necessarily, a unity and a whole, which cannot be dissolved into unknown quantities, and which exists as a whole or not at all; he grasps his metaphysical essence, spirit in transcendence and freedom. And from this transcendental analysis of what is said implicitly about man in every human act, he must then go on to see many other things as "essential" to man; his being in the world, his bodiliness, his belonging to a community of fellow men. In short, there is a metaphysical knowledge of man's essence, primarily here, of his nature, by the light of his reason, meaning independent of revelation; but also through a means (his reason) which is itself a part of the essence thus grasped. But for the theological reasons already given, it is also true that the actual human nature which is here experiencing itself need not, and cannot, regard all that it thus experiences as "pure" nature, as distinct from supernatural (particularly if this self-experience of man is seen in the context of the whole of human history, without which it cannot reach full awareness). Actual human nature is *never* "pure" nature, but nature in a supernatural order, which man (even the unbeliever and the sinner) can never escape from; nature superformed (which does not mean justified) by the supernatural saving grace offered to it. And these "existential facts" of his concrete (his "historical") nature are not just accidents of his being beyond his consciousness but make themselves apparent in his experience of himself. He cannot clearly distinguish them by simple reflection (by the light of natural reason) from the natural spirituality of his nature. But when once he knows through revelation that this order of grace exists, which is given to him unmerited and does not belong to his nature itself, then he will be more careful; he must take into account that perhaps many things which he concretely experiences in himself and ascribes almost involuntarily to his "nature" are in fact due to the working in him of what he knows from theology to be unmerited grace. Not as if he now no longer knew what was nature in him. The nature of a spiritual being and its supernatural elevation are not like two things laid one beside the other, or one against the other, which must either be kept separate or the one exchanged for the other. The supernatural elevation of man is the absolute (although unmerited) fulfilment of a being which, because of its spirituality and transcendence towards infinite being, cannot be "defined", i.e., "confined", like sub-human beings. These are "defined" through its being of their very essence to be limited to a particular sphere of reality. (It would therefore be impossible, for example, for them to be "elevated" to a super-natural fulfilment; this elevation would take away their essence which essentially "confines" them.) The "definition" of the created spirit is its open-ness to infinite being; it is a creature because of its openness to the fullness of reality; it is a spirit because it is open to reality *as such*, infinite reality. So it is not surprising that the greatness of the fulfilment—the openness does not of itself *require* this absolute and unsurpassable fulfilment and has a meaning without it—cannot be immediately recognized as either "owing" or "unmerited". Nevertheless, in spite of the difficulty in dis-tinguishing what is "nature" and what isn't, nature is not thereby overthrown. The beginnings of this fulfilment already exist—the experience of infinite longing, radical optimism, discontent which cannot find rest, anguish at the in-sufficiency of material things, protest against death, the experience of being the object of a love whose absoluteness and whose silence our mortality cannot bear, the experience of funda-mental guilt with hope nevertheless remaining etc. Because these beginnings are brought to absolute fulfilment by the power of God's grace, this means that in them we experience *both* grace *and* nature.

For we experience our nature where we experience grace; grace is only experienced where by nature there is spirit. And vice versa, in fact, as things are, when spirit is experienced it is a supernaturally elevated spirit. As long as we keep these remarks about the relationship between nature and grace to the general and formal, no particular difficulty arises, although we are saying that we can only encounter nature as spirit in the supernatural order and never the spirit as "pure nature". But it becomes more difficult when we try and make precise statements on the concrete and individual level. What, precisely, in this nature is nature, and what would not be there but for its elevation to the supernatural order? For example, is the resurrection of the body part of man's natural destiny as a spiritual person, or does it only happen through grace? Or what would the final destiny of a pure nature be like in the *concrete*? These are questions which could only be answered if we could experiment with pure nature, and use our results as the basis of a theory of its final destiny.[1] But as things are we cannot go beyond an essentially formal doctrine of a "natural" final destiny which—as from what

[1] If this nature's infinite openness *could* have a final destiny at all and not be, in the concrete, either the free limitation by God to a finite end, determined by him but which could not have been deduced *a priori* from the nature itself, *or* absolute fulfilment.

has been said is naturally to be expected—is merely an abstract formalization of the concrete doctrine of a supernatural final destiny. This goes to show that medieval theology did well not to bother too much about a natural beatitude. Not only because there is in fact no such thing, but also because it is basically only the abstract formalization of the actual supernatural final destiny taught by theology (and not so very helpful), and because if an attempt is made to make it concrete, it is bound to borrow unjustifiably from theology.

In fact this "pure" philosophy of man's natural essence is not even necessary. If we are talking to a non-Catholic we have only to remember not to base our argument on revealed facts which he does not accept. If in this conversation we refer to a man's experience of himself, we must note at once what the non-Christian does not accept in this experience. If he will not accept it on a certain point then it may be that he himself is not capable of a legitimately "natural" experience, either because he has been badly instructed or because in spite of good instruction he cannot grasp it by reflection (although he has it), or it may be that *we* are speaking of an experience which was in fact through grace, and the non-Christian's experience is not as clear as ours (he has it, though, in some measure, as we said above) and so he cannot understand our argument.

Because both cases are possible, because it is not easy even for a Christian to distinguish clearly between them, and because a supernatural argument can be meaningful and successful even with a non-Christian (when an argument from revelation is not possible), the question whether a metaphysical (i.e., pre-theological) argument has as its real starting-point "pure" nature or historical nature is in the concrete case of no great importance.

The concept of pure nature is a legitimate one. If someone says: I experience myself as a being which is unconditionally directed towards the immediate possession of God, he has not necessarily said anything untrue. The statement is only untrue if he says that this unconditional longing belongs to "pure" nature or if he says that this pure nature (which does not exist) *can't* exist. When a man knows through revelation that the Beatific Vision is through grace, and experiences it in his longing for it as a miracle of God's gratuitous love, he has to say that it is a free gift, not due to him by nature, not pledged to him by his creation (so that our creation, which was a free act of God, not due to us, and the free gift of grace to the already existing creature, are not one and the same gift of God's freedom). The concept of "pure nature" is implicit in this statement. It is not just a meaningless extravagance of idle theological speculation, but it is the necessary

background against which to see the Beatific
Vision as free grace, not due to us; not due to us
either as sinners or as creatures.

The attempt to work out more clearly the way
in which nature is ordered to grace (in the sense
of a *potentia oboedentialis*) is still meaningful
when we realize that grace is not due to nature,
whether sinful or not. This does not make it necessary to think of this *potentia oboedentialis* for
grace more or less as the mere lack of contradiction to it, with the resulting "extrinsicity" already
spoken of. Being ordered to grace and being
directed to grace in such a way that without the
actual gift of this grace it would all be meaningless, are not the same thing. Even though a spirit
(i.e., openness to God, freedom and conscious and
free self-possession) is essentially impossible without this transcendence, whose *absolute* fulfilment
is grace, yet *this* fulfilment does not thereby become due; supposing, of course, that the conscious
self-possession in freedom is itself meaningful in
God's sight (and not just a means, a mere phase
on the way, towards possessing the Beatific
Vision). This supposition is perfectly legitimate.
For the absolute (not infinite) worth and validity
in itself of every personal act makes this supposition. If it is legitimate, then this is how things
stand: Without transcendence open to the supernatural there is no spirit; but spirit itself is already
meaningful without supernatural grace. Its fulfil-

ment through grace is not, therefore, an exigency
of its nature, although it is open to this supernatural fulfilment. And when this is clear we are
no longer in danger of forgetting the supernaturalness of grace, and can proceed without further
hindrance to work out with all due precision the
exact meaning of this transcendence of the spirit
towards the supernatural. We can only fully
understand man in his "undefinable" essence if
we see him as *potentia oboedentialis* for the divine
life; this is his *nature*. His nature is such that its
*absolute* fulfilment comes through grace, and so
nature *of itself* must reckon with the *meaningful*
possibility of remaining without absolute fulfilment. The attempt can even be made to see the
Hypostatic Union in the line of this absolute
fulfilment of what man actually is. Going into
all this in order to try and get a metaphysical
anthropology as close as possible to the teaching
on grace and to see the higher as the gratuitous
fulfilment of the lower,[1] is not just idle playing
about. If we don't do this it will not be possible
in the long run to awaken in people an existential
interest in that mysterious life which is given with
supernatural grace. In the working out of the full

[1] Everywhere in the hierarchically constructed universe
of real differences without "jumps"—with the many and
different coming out of the one—"fulfilment" and
"gratuitousness" both in one are the characteristic mark
of the relationship between two realities.

and precise meaning of the term *potentia oboedentialis* we should not confine our attention too
one-sidedly (as often happens) to human *knowledge*. In Scripture God is love and not *gnosis
gnoseos*; we can therefore only fully understand
man and his absolute fulfilment (through grace) if
we see him as freedom and love—and this not
only as the complement and emotional accom-
paniment of knowledge. For reasons already
given it is not at all a bad thing that in this
analysis of man as *potentia oboedentialis* there
has been no "chemically pure" description of pure
nature, but mixed in with it there are traces of
elements of historical nature, i.e., nature possessing grace. Who is to say that the voice heard in
earthly philosophy, even non-Christian and pre-
Christian philosophy, is the voice of nature alone
(and perhaps of nature's guilt) and not also the
groaning of the creature, who is already moved in
secret by the Holy Spirit of grace, and longs without realizing it for the glory of the children of God?

There is still much more to be said on the subject of the present state of the theology of grace,
what it is and what it should be. We should discuss grace in its relationship to the Church,[1] what

[1] H. de Lubac, *Catholicism. A Study of the corporate
destiny of mankind*, trans. Lancelot Sheppard (from the
4th edition of *Catholicisme. Les Aspects sociaux du
dogme*, Paris, 1947), London, 1950.

it means and how it is ordered to society; the current textbooks tend to treat it with a curiously individualistic narrowness. And we should mention the renewed interest in the relationship between grace and man's personal action. But there is no more room for this here.

Little advances and shifts in the field of the theory of any science are often not of immediately evident importance. At first these changes may look like mere passing fashions or scholarly quibbling. But if we realize that these new insights enter the common consciousness and become the unquestioned suppositions which are the basis for our action, then we may begin to see that a great deal, sometimes everything, depends on them. It is a strange thing that we Christians are often convinced enough of the power of "theory" to produce very practical results; but by "theory" we are not so likely to mean theology as Church politics, social questions, propaganda methods and suchlike. Living theology itself is not very highly thought of. Many people in the Church often have the impression that it goes on fussing superfluously with questions which were settled long ago, causes disturbances and keeps people from attending to more important things. These people do not realize that a lively and inquiring theology of today is working to make tomorrow's preaching reach mind and heart. This work of theology's may often look inconsequential and fruitless. But it is necessary. Even though heart and grace are the only things which we cannot do without.

# PART 2

# DANGERS IN CATHOLICISM TODAY

# INTRODUCTION

THE greatest dangers are always so particularly dangerous because they go unnoticed. It is the same in the Church. She is always threatened by dangers. The greatest are those from within; all those from outside only become dangerous to her if they touch upon a weakness within. The promise that the gates of hell will never prevail against the Church does not promise her constant visible, "empirical" strength and immunity, but promises the power which is God's alone in the weakness and vulnerability of the men who are her members. When men feel safe and assured because "nothing can ever really happen to the Church", then they always find out sooner or later that indeed nothing can "happen" to the *Church*, who is in God's hand, but quite a lot can happen to the men who out of idleness or timidity do nothing and rely on this. The dangers to the Church are often unnoticed—the spirit of an age, for example, which is taken for granted everywhere, and so also in the heart and instincts of the good and faithful Christian before he can control it with an understanding armed with the truths of the Faith; the spirit of an age, which can

even secretly be at work in those who are protest-
ing against it. (For example rationalism is fought
very rationalistically, because one must "fight one's
opponent with his own weapons".) These dangers
can always only be overcome by the saints and
prophets of the Church. For only they can con-
quer through the ever-new (and ever-ancient) Holy
Spirit, the spirit of a new age "non in persuasi-
bilibus humanae sapientiae verbis, sed in osten-
sione spiritus et virtutis". They overcome this
spirit not by arguing against it (even though in
the household of the Church this, too, is unavoid-
able), but by bringing and manifesting to it in
themselves the eternal Holy Spirit of the Church
so powerfully that he becomes the living Spirit of
the day. (How little and humble these beginnings
often are, and how old-fashioned and outdated
they can seem!) We others, in our fight against
these dangers, use the weapons of human wisdom;
we argue in a harassed way about this and that;
we try to immunize against diseases without being
able to get out of the country in which the disease
is endemic; we fight with the weapons of our
opponents and we can count ourselves lucky if
they don't do us more harm than the enemy; we
fight for God's truth (we do really), and in doing
so always defend a little (unnoticed and against
our will) our own error, which is of yesterday,
against the error of today. And when we are
finished we find with shame that we have been

God's unprofitable servants. But we can comfort ourselves that even this fight by humble servants and miserable sinners was also God's will, as long as we realize that it is not a question of our saving his Church but of his saving us in her.

The three essays gathered together here are not the call of a prophet. They do not claim to point out *the* dangers—either all of them or the most important—to the Church today or to strike down the greatest and most widespread dangers by the manifestation of the Spirit and his power. They are three essays which originally appeared in different places, and no effort has been made to disguise their origin. They are essays of a theology teacher. A little abstract, therefore, and pedantic, as befits his subject (today at any rate). They approach their common subject in different ways; in one the danger is reviewed by setting out some positive principles; in another the danger in question is described mainly *a posteriori* and a little said about how to deal with it; in the third the danger is in a sense deduced *a priori* and not much said about fighting it.

At any rate, here are three dangers which it is perhaps worth the trouble of thinking about. They hang closely together. The danger in the first chapter is the opposite to that in the second chapter: in the one the danger of the individual taking refuge in the collective and thinking that to be a good and mature Christian it is enough to march willingly and stoutly with all the rest in the mass of the "people of the Church"; in the other, the danger of making moral decisions only as a unique individual and thinking one has no obligation to obey the universal law which the Church is and which she preaches (as a law of love and true freedom). The third chapter turns from the general danger of a false idea of individuality to the individual case of the Church's teaching and speaks of the danger of esoteric theories about this which are against the very nature of the Church's faith and her teaching authority.

# 1

## THE INDIVIDUAL IN THE CHURCH

NYONE who has to speak about the individual in the Church today has a difficult task before him. He may well still be able to say something "quite correct". But will he be able to say the *decisive* thing for the time in which we live? We are in the midst of a tremendous battle between an individualism which is centuries old, and the new collectivism which is advancing victoriously, secure in the knowledge that the future is in its hands. And we Christians are divided against ourselves; for the noise of our own arguments against individualism, subjectivism, the individual and his independent rights, is still ringing in our ears and now a new age is upon us which has laid the old world in its grave, and we regretfully remember what a good time we had in that world which we fought so hard against. And when we carefully take up a middle position between the two, a polemical "neither-nor" and a synthetic "both-and", don't we perhaps have an uneasy feeling that our formula is very nice—but very theoretical?

We can't say that this difficulty is about things which do not concern us, that we are not concerned with the individual and the community in general, but with the individual and the religious community of the Church. It is true that in this case we can have a surer knowledge of the theoretical relationship between them. It is true that here it could at least seem that the practical difficulty for actual living people were only one-sided: the question of the Christian and his rights as opposed to the rights of the Christian community, so that we should be back to our apologetics for the social against the individual. But if we look more carefully we find that the atmosphere of the general conflict between individual and community is the same as in our conflict. When, in the last three hundred years, the individual would have nothing to do with the Church, this was because of a general basic attitude of individualism which he, who had absorbed the intellectual life of the preceding three hundred years, would share and which would make him passionately defend the rights of the individual against the claims of the community. And so it comes that our problem shares in the general uncertainty of the whole field. The latest statements, with their formal "both-and" and "partly-partly", may be clear. They are clear. This is important and encouraging. But can we be so completely certain that the individualism of the past few centuries—perhaps since the end of the Middle Ages—has not also done its work—even when all basic principles have been adhered to—in the Church and among good and faithful Christians, work which was permissible, perhaps even right, for the time, and yet also, perhaps, here and there exaggerated, even harmful? Can we be sure that we know how to strike the exact balance between the individual and the community, even if we *are* agreed on the theoretical principles? Are we certain that the actual daily life of the Church, past and present, has not ever laid a burden on the individual of today which we have no right to ask him to bear? And finally, aren't we now seeing a failure of the individual good practising Catholic in his duty to make decisions which is his precisely *as* an individual, while he looks inquiringly to the Church for directives which are either, unfortunately, in fact not given, or which could not be given at all and so should not be expected, a passive do-nothing attitude because no directive has been given from above? And doesn't this force us to realize that in the Church too there is a sheep-like submissiveness and anti-individualistic self-effacement which we, who battled so fiercely against individualism, did not bargain for, and which should terrify us? And are we not already witnessing here and there among faithful Catholics a decline in private religious practices, moral self-discipline, ascesis etc., even though they take part wholeheartedly in the communal religious life of the Church? And so isn't there a need for an examination and defence of the individual in the Church, of his rights and above all his duties in relation to the Church as a body? Aren't we, then, involved within the Church in a war on two fronts? How to conform the individual to the Church and the Church to the individual? Isn't the situation here just as confused and difficult as in the general conflict between the individual and society in the secular sphere? What is the right thing for us to concentrate on *today*?

What follows does not claim to give the final answer to these questions. Its purpose is more modest. It is limited to the theoretical, abstract and general. It speaks theoretical truths, and sometimes only theoretical opinions, in the hope that for a start even this may be of some use.

## I. THE INDIVIDUAL

The first point to be made is twofold: There is, and there should be, an individual in the religious sphere. What does this mean and why is it so?

### 1. PHILOSOPHICAL AND DOGMATIC VIEW OF THE INDIVIDUAL

It is impossible to elaborate here a metaphysic and ontology of the individual, and even if we did, it could not hope to obtain general acceptance. For as long as there is a *philosophia perennis* it will remain at variance on this question. Only a brief general outline can be sketched, which, although its Thomist origin is still evident, is so preliminary to an exact philosophical statement and system, that it will be acceptable to any Christian philosophy.

The concept "individual" is difficult to define. It is not the genuine, exclusive opposite to "common", but, rather, correlative to it, and increases and decreases *with* it. All the mistakes in this field arise from the failure to realize the analogical and correlative character of these concepts. They only conflict and exclude each other when individuality on a certain level declares itself an absolute, and is opposed to a correlative "community" which is on a completely different level of being. If, for example, individuality on the spiritual-personal level raises itself to an absolute ideal, and from this pinnacle on which it has set itself decides what community may still keep on the level of society or the group (the correlative to individuality on the material level), then you have individualism. Or, when individuality on the material-biological level is rightly seen (for it does exist), but then correlated to community on the spiritual-personal level, then you have collectivism. Individuality does not always mean the same thing; what makes a thing an individual being, a being existing for itself which cannot be substituted or exchanged, is by no means always the same. At the lowest end of the scale is the merely

individuated single being which must pay for
being "in itself" by being enclosed within itself,
excluding everything else, and which cannot go
out from itself without ceasing to possess even
its own action, making it into something outside
itself which it acts *upon*. At the highest is the
greatest mystery of our Faith, the most perfect
individuality, who, in the fullest sense, exists for
his own sake and is immutable, but nevertheless
excludes nothing of the perfection of any other
being, having all reality within himself; who gives
himself totally and yet for this very reason possesses himself most completely; in whom perfect
individuality and perfect community do not conflict but *are* each other. Between these two ex-
tremes, the one the "death" of lifeless matter and
the other the infinite life of the Blessed Trinity, is
man. He is rooted in earth, individuated, and thus
separated from others, by matter, in which there
is neither true individuality nor true community,
because the individuality is the same kind as every
other man's and the community merely the sum
total of all its component individuals. But through
the liberating individuality of a spiritual personality he can also come to share in the life of
the Trinity, that most perfect community and
most radical individuality which belong to the
Father, the Son and the Holy Ghost. And because
man is body, spirit and grace, and because he is
all this in his individuality, neither he nor it can

be reduced to a rigid formula. He has the individuality of all levels of being; he contains within him all the Protean changeableness of the world itself.

He is an individual by *matter*, that is, an individual by demarcation from many more like him; *a* man, one individuated human being (for only mankind can be man as a whole); and he is merely an individual who is one among many more, one example of countless others, so common that he is just one more like the rest, of no particular importance, and so all by himself and lonely.

However, he is at the same time a *spiritual* personality. That is, he is more than an individual example of many more the same, more than one individuation of a common kind. He is a genuine individual, who is truly unique and irreplaceable, and who, when he comes into contact with another, does not form a society or group of like beings, but a community of different, unique beings. For in spite of, or rather because of his spiritual-personal uniqueness and "unexchangeability", he is open to infinite reality by knowledge and love, and by this knowing and loving-valuing openness he can *become* all things—even the other *as* other—and, vice versa, he can only become all things in so far as he becomes spiritual and personal, that is, a unique individual.

Furthermore, man is a *son of God*. That is, if we may bring theology into this examination of

3

the analogy of individuality, God his creator
values him so highly as a unique individual, that
he has given him the power to enter the community of the most perfect individuality; by grace
he can become the beloved child of the Father
together with his only-begotten Son, and with the
Son call the Father *his* Father; and with the Holy
Ghost he can lovingly embrace both Father and
Son, and thus receive an individuality in grace
and glory which is a supernatural sharing in the
individuality of the Trinity. In other words, individuality (the *unum* of scholasticism) is a transcendental concept, and goes together with the
concept of "existing being" and, like this concept,
has analogical meanings. If, then, an existing
being's measure of individuality is determined by
its analogical degree of being, the degree of being
of a man in grace and glory can only be determined by uncreated grace, that is, by the communication to him, by grace but really, of God
himself in his own reality; and so this is man's
highest and finally determining individuality, and
it is itself determined from within by the individuality of the three divine persons of the Trinity.
He shares by grace in the individuality of God,
which is a perfect community in possession of an
identical reality.

But these three levels of individuality must be
seen as they belong together united in the one
man. Each of these descriptions of one level is

only true if it is seen in union with the others, each of these three levels only becomes a reality when, in the unity of the human person, it comes into contact with the others. Man becomes a member of the species when he gets his spiritual personality, and he only gets this by becoming a member of the species. The same goes for the relationships to others corresponding to each of these three levels of individuality, society or group which correspond to material, biological individuality; community which is the correlative to spiritual, personal individuality; union in Christ (as we can say, following Gal. 3.28), which is the correlative to theological individuality—none can ever be isolated from the other levels, above or below. And because of this, the group, for example, is not just a herd; although it belongs ontologically to the sphere of material-biological individuality with its corresponding multiplicity of like beings, it can, through man's spiritual, personal action, be made truly human. And likewise, man's spiritual-personal community is not an angel-like heavenly hierarchy, but needs, in order to be itself, the media which belong to the material-biological sphere and so to the group. If individuality and membership of a community are not conflicting but complementary concepts, then the real problem is not whether man is an individual or a member of a community, nor is it really that human individuality, and so human community, are themselves on three levels, to which the one word "individual" applies only in an analogical sense. The really difficult problem is to find the right balance and the true recognition of each other between individuality on one level and community on the *other* levels. We shall see more clearly what this means when we consider the concrete case of the relationship between the Church as a society, on the level of the group, and the individual as a spiritual-personal being who also possesses a supernatural life.

## 2. RELIGIOUS VIEW OF THE INDIVIDUAL

The Christian religion recognizes the individual. In fact, it was the first, in the true sense, to discover him. Ancient classical philosophy regarded only the universal and eternally unchanging as eternal and of any real importance. And so when pagans thought most deeply about their gods, they saw even them as no more than unseeing representations of universal norms subordinate, in the last resort, to the impersonal *dike* and *heimarmene*. Christianity, on the other hand, recognizes the individual. He *as* an individual, has a unique, eternally important destiny; during a limited space of time with a real beginning and a real end, he makes himself what he will be for eternity. In the Christian religion, *each man* can call the Infinite One *his* God, a God who in his turn calls each man by name and in spite of his infinity acts in each case in a free, unrepeatable and incalculable way; for universal norms are not finally decisive with him, but to each of his creatures, in that private, unrepeatable dialogue which we call grace, he gives a unique love which is for him alone. Each man is to go into his room and shut the door and pray to him in secret as his God; he gives himself by grace to each directly, without anything whatever coming between, and this in spite of, or rather *because of*, the mediation of all grace through Christ the mediator and his church, whose purpose is not to come between God and man in the manner of the neo-Platonic or Areopagitical cosmic hierarchy of mediators, but to give each man immediate access to God. When Paul says, "He loved me and gave himself for me"; or when Pascal speaks of the Lord saying, "J'ai versé telle goute de sang pour toi"; or when Newman speaks continually of "God and myself", this is just common Christian knowledge of the absolute eternal importance of each individual.

## 3. ETHICAL AND MORAL-THEOLOGICAL VIEW OF THE INDIVIDUAL

If the ontological structure of a being determines how it should behave, then a human being is morally bound to be and become by the exercise of his free choice the individual he is. As a spiritual-personal being and a sharer by grace in the life of the Trinity he has an individuality which is really unique and unexchangeable, never accidental or conformed to a set pattern. This spiritual and personal uniqueness is not subject to universal norms, laws and rules, but nevertheless, like everything else, is still under the binding will of God, which in this case is not for the individual as one of a common kind, but from person to person, from God to each single man. And so there is a sphere of individual morality and religion, a sphere of moral duties and religious objectives which, while it never conflicts with the universal moral law, nevertheless has the decisive word over and above it and can no longer be contained within it. Of course there is not, and must not be, an individual morality which sets itself up against the universal moral law; but there is an individual morality which is binding on the individual as uniquely for him, and this cannot be called a mere application of a universal principle to one case. And so there is a "private" sphere of moral and religious life which universal morality and its expounders and guardians do not merely in fact overlook, but which is by its very nature out of their reach.

This private sphere is thus not in the least a sphere of arbitrary choice and freedom from obligations, but is directly subject to the morally binding holy will of God. God of course wills precisely that each man should be a unique individual, and this uniqueness he not only received at his creation but is free himself to achieve throughout his life; it can, and by its nature must, be the object not only of God's creating will but also of his morally binding will. There is a power in many which recognizes this individual morality as its obligatory norm. When we call it conscience we must distinguish between two functions of conscience; the one which tells a man's subjective self the *universal* norms of ethics and moral theology and applies them to his "case", and the one by which the individual hears God's call to him *alone*, which can never be fully deduced from universal norms. There must therefore be a "technique" or, better still, a *techne*, an "art" in the Greek sense, of apprehending the demands of this strict individual morality, and this is to be clearly distinguished from the theory, the *episteme*, establishing the universally valid norms of moral philosophy and theology. If we were to look for a traditional name for it we would call it the charismatic art of "discernment of spirits", a term which, during the last few hundred years, has in fact usually been misunderstood because the discernment was either expressly or implicitly understood to be limited to the perfection of the casuistical application of theoretical norms to the individual "case". Really it is something quite different; it is the ability to hear and recognize God's call to this man alone among the many voices all calling him in different directions, the "spirits". What follows from this will immediately be seen when we now consider the relationship between the individual we have thus defined and the Church.

## II. THE INDIVIDUAL IN THE CHURCH

### 1. THE CHURCH

Before we can state more precisely the relationship between this individual and the Church we must first say a little about the Church's nature as it concerns us here. The Church is the community of the redeemed bound together in spirit in Christ Jesus, and at the same time a visible organized society with rules and founder's charter. Neither truth about the Church should be separated from or confused with the other. If we saw in the Church only the union in Christ by grace of the redeemed, this would be the heresy of a purely invisible Church; if we saw in her only the organized society, the "Ministry of Salvation", this would be ecclesiological Nestorianism, as Leo XIII called it, or, as Pius XII called it, ecclesiological naturalism. Both these realities belong to the Church's fullness; in a certain way the one is a sacramental visibility signifying the other; but nevertheless they do not fully overlap, it is not possible to think of them as strictly two aspects of one and the same thing which cannot exist apart. For, to mention only the least disputable case, under certain circumstances someone can belong to the community-by-grace of the redeemed in Christ without being a member of the visible, organized Church. And—this is in fact dogma—someone can be a member of the visible society of the Church and yet be cut off from the community in Christ through mortal sin, which can even be a purely internal denial of the Faith. And so community by grace and the organized society, although they are ordered to one another and belong together in the fullness of the Church, are distinct realities and in different sociological spheres, and constituted differently. Consequently the relationships of the individual to the Church as a community and to the Church as a society are not the same.

The Church as a community by grace in Christ is in the same sphere as, and is correlative to, spiritual and personal individuality elevated by grace; the Church as an organized society is correlative to the individual as a materially, biologically individuated member of a species, who thus ontologically can and must be subject to a law, which is the same for him and his fellows, authority imposed from without, dominating influences etc.

As we said before, the real difficulty lies only in the relationship between the Church as an organized society and man as a spiritual and personal individual. This is what we must discuss further. We have already made plain and need not repeat that even man's unique and unrepeatable personal individuality is not that of an individualism which would make him alone, but makes him one of the great community of countless unique spiritual persons and one of the union by grace in Christ. In what follows, when we speak of the Church we shall always mean the Church as an organized hierarchical body, the Church who, through laws, commands, general directives etc., guides and supports men in working out their salvation. When we speak of the individual we always mean man in his spiritual and personal individuality, not as just one of the species.

## 2. THE INDIVIDUAL IN THE CHURCH

We hope that now the essential point which we are here concerned with is clear; in every man there is a sphere of personal individuality elevated by grace which we may call *private* and which cannot and may not be touched by the Church. Not as if this sphere were not also Christian, that is, conformed to Christ and superformed by grace; on the contrary. Not as if this sphere were a sphere of private arbitrary choices and of freedom from moral obligation to God; not as if, for this sphere, laws could not be formulated (right up to the three divine persons whom we "count together") or general and analogical statements be made (and unfortunately must be). Not as if one part of man was out of the Church's reach, for because of his unique nature and the resulting interpenetration of his metaphysical levels of being, she reaches indirectly even his spiritual and personal uniqueness, his "private" sphere. But within the Church he has a truly private sphere, in the sense that this cannot be immediately reached by the Church as a lawgiving society. This private sphere is, as we said, private *in principle*, essentially private, private by nature. In every society there are some things, some actions of its members, which *in fact*, because of their unimportance, are not objects of the society's authority and are left to the individual, even though (of course this might be very difficult or impossible in practice) they could be subject to the society's authority. But this is a private sphere *beneath* the society's authority, as we might say. It must not be confused with the private sphere *above* it or secret from it, which it cannot and may not touch. There is, for example, no ruling by the Church as to how much incense should be put in the censer; there is no ruling as to what the individual should say to his God in his private prayers. But these two cases are fundamentally different. The word "sphere" must further be guarded against misunderstanding, because in our ontological analysis we are dealing with *meta-*

*physical* levels of being in man which are conceptually, not really, distinct (although they are partly founded on the real distinction between body and soul). The private sphere is, of course, *not* necessarily a clearly delimitable real region the region of "purely internal acts") which is materially and visibly delimited from the social sphere. But because man is also a unique spiritual and personal being, elevated by grace, he must have in his total human activity a private sphere in which spirit and grace can be actualized and expressed. In other words, because in his *being* he is made up of more than one metaphysical component, and all must be realized and expressed, in his *doing*, which is always done by his whole self, the principles of action corresponding to these metaphysical levels of being, and the organs of these principles, must forbearingly make room for each other so that they can all fulfil themselves.

And so it is not to be expected that particular acts of a man, which are always acts of the whole man, can be clearly seen beforehand to be out of the reach of ecclesiastical-social authority. And yet the principle is sound that there must be actions which affirm the spiritual-supernaturalized uniqueness of man and the limits which the Church as a society ascribes to herself. Thus there can and should be actions which are the expression of a man's personal and Christian uniqueness, although they are in themselves also accessible to ecclesiastical authority. If the preceding reasoning is sound, then we have shown that this must be true. But we must consider a few facts which will enable us to put it more precisely, illustrate it and show its implications so that we can see what it means in practical pastoral terms.

First we must consider that the Church recognizes and respects this sphere. She claims authority to rule and even to punish the individual. But she has never claimed the right to decide finally his moral standing in the sight of God. We see that this is true not merely because it would in practice be very difficult, but because there is in fact no ecclesiastical "human judgement day" by which a man can finally be judged. (1 Cor. 4.5.) In moral theology there is the famous disputed question, which has not even yet been settled, as to whether the Church can directly command internal acts. However it is eventually settled—as we have shown, this is of no importance for our present question—it at least shows that in moral theology there is the implicit awareness that we may not take for granted that the Church can claim the right to rule and command every part of a man. We could consider the fact that the Church herself forgoes the right to force the Faith and baptism upon the unbaptized, and we could ask ourselves what principles govern her behaviour

in this respect which would apply also to the
baptized. For the difference between them is not
of such a kind that there is no limit to the
authority of the Church over the baptized, because without any doubt she has a right to make
demands in the name of God on the unbaptized
also.

Finally we must consider this: A large part of
a Christian's religious life is, at least in fact, outside the official juridical life of the Church. There
is, at least in fact, a private religious life. What the
Christian thinks, reads and prays, which religious
vocations he chooses, which way to Christian perfection he follows etc., is left to his own decision.
For Christians in general the religious duties as
members of the society of the Church are very
light; Sunday Mass, fasting laws, Easter duties etc.
Is this merely because it is the Church's policy to
restrict the duties she imposes on her members?
Is it because the rest belongs to the "private sphere
beneath", as we called it? Or can we see from this
the fundamental fact that there must be a real,
original "private sphere above" in religion too?
Without any doubt this last is true. Otherwise we
should have to admit that the Church *should*
exercise a religious dictatorship or collectivism
over this sphere, that she should set up an obligatory ecclesiastical appointments office to decide
everyone's vocation in the Church under pain of
sin, decide who are to be priests, which women

are to be parish helpers, who are to be on the parish council. Or that she should control the length and content of everybody's prayers, even if this were a practical possibility. To ask questions like these is to answer them immediately in the negative. This means that there must be a private sphere in the Church which in principle and by nature cannot be regimented and fulfilled by the Church as a society. We can't say that this is accepted as a matter of course. Are we sure that in our practical dealings we never forget it, so long as we have not also worked it out theoretically?

And so now at last we come to what we actually set out to do; to try and illustrate the abstract principle and bring out its implications so that we can show what it means in practical pastoral terms.

### III. CONCLUSIONS AND APPLICATIONS

When we call the private religious sphere the region in which man's spiritual-personal and supernatural individuality must express and realize itself, we can see for ourselves what we need to consider when we speak of the individual in the Church.

(1) Because the individual is a unique spirit-person, in religious matters too he has *the right and the duty to make choices* which cannot be

directly governed by the Church's laws. We have already spoken about the individual morality which is a duty for us all, and about the individual function of conscience which does not subject the individual to universal laws but directs the moral choices possible to him through his spiritual individuality, which is not merely that by which he is one of the species. Now we must expressly add that *this individual morality cannot be directly governed by the Church*. Of course the Church can preach a formal kind of individual morality— become who you are; fulfil God's will for you as an individual—but she cannot tell me what I am actually meant to be. Of course the Church says, be the individual you are in the sight of God. But she cannot tell a man exactly—and in this case exactness is everything—what he is, what he must do to be this individual. This is not just a negative statement about the Church. When we say the Church may not and does not want, as Dostoievsky puts it in his story of the Grand Inquisitor, to relieve the individual of the burden and the duty of having to be an individual, this implies an imperative for *him*; he is not allowed at all times to take shelter behind the moral rulings of the Church. He is not necessarily clear in his conscience if there is no directive; he is not necessarily justified before God even if he has kept all the laws expressible in abstract terms. Over and above the Commandments preached by the

Church he has still to ask: Lord, what do you want *me* to do? He must know that moral theology and casuistry, however necessary they both may be, are no substitute for the gift of discernment of spirits in the sense we explained before; there must be in him and for him a fundamentally private life of prayer and moral decisions. The man who misuses Church and liturgical community as a way of escaping from himself is an ecclesiastical collectivist and belongs to the sheeplike mob described in the story of the Grand Inquisitor, who think they are saved when they are freed *from* themselves—instead of to themselves—by the Church relieving them of the burden of having to take initiative and make decisions.

At the moment collectivism is the order of the day; but for us it is at its most dangerous not in the compulsory collectivism which assails the Church from outside, but in the collectivism inside the Church, our own weariness and idleness which gladly forgoes the responsibility of making decisions. When we are sometimes surprised at people's good will towards the Church and her directives, the leadership of her priests and youth organizers—at least, peoples who are still in regions sociologically Catholic—we should not always be entirely pleased about it; it can also mean an attitude of collectivism, a good will which is not through the power of faith and a vital, carefully considered personal conviction, but a weakness of will which has so little courage and belief in itself that it is ready to follow anyone who is prepared to lead, and in this case it may be the priest because for purely sociological reasons (family tradition, political loyalty etc.), he may be the most immediately obvious leader. But only brave hearts can really be won for God. Isn't, for example, the noticeable disappearance of a private thanksgiving after Communion such a sign of a collectivist tendency among people who immediately become spiritually breathless when they are left alone to pray? When someone cannot pray by himself at a private Low Mass, this at any rate seems to indicate something of the kind.

A few years ago we were always talking about the "adulthood" of the laity. When this was used to imply that the individualist should be able to do whatever he wanted, when it implied ill-feeling against the many exactly formulated rules of divine and ecclesiastical moral law, when it became a slogan with which to attack an unwelcome clarity and unambiguousness in moral law and casuistry, even when this was obviously possible with practically no difficulty, it was all a big mistake. Where universal norms are possible they cannot be appealed against in the name of individual conscience. If induced abortion or contraception can be universally recognized as morally wrong and are declared to be morally wrong by

the Church, then there is no appeal against this
in the name of individual conscience; as long as
it is something objectively right the universal norm
must be repeatedly taught to the individual so
that he won't go against it. But *within* the morally
possible and allowable in the abstract, there is a
field of individual obligation and individual duty.
And this is also the field for the "adult" laity.
For example, a certain form of devotion to our
Lady could in certain circumstances not be imposed as a duty for everybody by the Church and
yet be an obligation and duty before God and his
conscience for an individual. Joan of Arc had a
duty to dress in men's clothes and fight for her
king and country, without being told so by the
Church. And the chief difficulty when her cause
was brought forward for canonization was not
whether in practice and in theory she was always
obedient to the commands of the Church, but
whether, even during her trial, she ever fell short
of this individual duty. Today the danger of an
ecclesiastical collectivism is hard upon us; not by
the Church overstepping her limits, but by the
individual not being able to hold out and bear his
responsibility any longer, and clinging onto the
Church's apron-strings; not by the Church wanting to reduce her members to servitude, but by the
masters themselves wanting to be enslaved.

It is, of course, not possible in the space of this
brief essay to say exactly how these imperatives of

individual morality are to be recognized in concrete cases. But after what we have said about the
individual one thing at least must be clear; an
individual imperative is not necessarily absent if
it cannot be exhaustively deduced from the universal moral law. This is an obvious fact which in
practice is extremely often forgotten. When in an
important question, we pray to the Holy Ghost,
as well as asking the moral theologians, we pray
*not only* that the moral theologians may be enlightened by him to apply the right rules rightly
to our case—this indeed is a difficult task in itself
and needs the help of prayer—but also that he
may tell us further what precisely he wants *us* to
do within what is morally possible. For very often
(in principle, that is, if not in practice always),
within this sphere there are several possibilities,
of which one is willed by God, and a failure to do
this one can have the most grievous consequences.
When at some future time it is asked whether we
Christians and the Church as she is on earth today
have done the right thing, they will not be able to
say of us that for the most part we have acted
theologically immorally, but perhaps they may
not be able to say so easily that we have done the
*will of God*. God has a particular will for each
individual but of course each individual will not
learn what it is in such an extraordinary way, by
a kind of revelation, as did Joan of Arc, Catherine
of Siena, Bernadette Soubirous and others like

these. How this "call" usually comes, how precisely this spiritual individual instinct works, how it is supported by the guidance of the Holy Ghost through his gifts, how it can be tested by the "art" of discernment of spirits, how more precisely an individual call like this to follow after Christ comes through reading Scripture and meditating on the life of Jesus (so that for us the life of Jesus is more than merely one case exemplifying the fulfilment of the moral law completely independent of him), all this is impossible to go into here. In this context we can only draw attention to one thing; however much it is for the individual himself to find out what he as an individual is meant to decide and do, we can and should help each other. To put it concretely, the spiritual director or confessor is more—or, in individual cases, should be more—than a practical moral theologian. Of course he must be a moral theologian too, for with good will he can learn moral theology, and God does not usually supply heavenly charismata to make up for our laziness and ignorance; but he should really be more than this; he should seek heavenly enlightenment with his penitent, pray with him to learn the will of God and not imagine he knows it all already just because he has worked hard at moral theology; he should be a sensitive reactor to impulses from God, he should be prepared to share the burden of making decisions, he should, in fact, be an enlightened "spiritual father" (which, of course, no-one can become just by having all the trappings of one).

(2) As this unique individuality is also on the level of *grace*, the individual's action is not only personal decision under God's unique will for him, but itself given by God by grace; this means that it is not only action raised by grace with power to share in God's life, but also *charismatic action*. Each man has his charisma, his gift, his vocation, says St. Paul. We must not always expect this to be something manifestly extraordinary or miraculous. In practice we cannot clearly distinguish it from the level of spiritual-personal individuality, which in itself still belongs to the natural sphere, even though it works itself out in the religious sphere too. And so for practical purposes we have already spoken about this charismatic vocation in what we said before. But we should also speak of it directly because it sheds light on our theme from another direction, immediately biblical. The charismatic in the Church is what is unique by grace in the Church, the individual's right by grace in the Church and for the Church. In the Church there is not only the institutional, universal and permanent; grace and impulsions to action come not only through the institutional sacraments, commandments and official guidance and ruling. God doesn't abdicate in favour of the Church and leave her to rule for

him undisturbed. Still today his Holy Spirit is at work directly in the Church, he is present in ever-new and unique events, and the direction in which he moves cannot be certainly predetermined by the law of the Church. The Church is not just a band of charismatics free to do whatever they will, but none the less, as Pius XII says in his encyclical, the charismatic—the element in her, if we may so put it, of dynamic unrest if not of revolutionary upheaval—belongs to her very essence. The Spirit of God, himself this holy un-rest making all things new, does not necessarily come upon the Church in her official rulers. Children, virgins and the poor in spirit can also become seers and prophets in the new alliance, and can learn from God a new way of being a Christian and a new Christian way of life, and can receive from him a mission to show this to the Church of their time . . . And the official Church and we members of the Church would do wrong if we were to refuse to listen to such a message, if we were to try and force such messages, im-pulsions, missions and charismata to choose strictly between being traditional and being false. It is a curious thing that those who would like to be charismatics themselves often immediately appeal to dogma and tradition when they are confronted with a genuine charismatic utterance which they ought to listen to, if it goes against their habits of thinking. Devotion to the Sacred

Heart, as Margaret Mary Alacoque proclaimed it,
was, whatever Richstätter and Hugo Rahner may
say to the contrary, genuinely "new" and so right;
it met a situation in the Church which was not
always there. What is true in big things is true in
small; and we should never forget the counsel
given by the *Spiritual Exercises* of St. Ignatius to
the director of exercises (who in a certain measure
is the Church's representative): "He is to allow the
Creator to deal with his creature and the creature
with his Creator *directly*." (*Annotatio* 15a.)
Wherever we have this "direct dealing", pre-
supposed by Ignatius to be a perfectly normal
preliminary, between the Lord and the individual
man, there we have the beginning of a genuine
charisma, however quiet and simple and unob-
trusive its first appearance may be.

(3) A third thing—already partly touched upon
—which we have still to say about this private
religious sphere in the Church is something about
our *relations with others within this sphere*, if we
may call it this.[1] The private sphere is not an
isolated region which does not come into contact
with the social at all. And because of this an
individual's private sphere can and should make
contact with others. Christians can and should be
bound together in a relationship which is not itself

---

[1] For what follows cf. Karl Rahner, "Friedliche
Erwägungen über das Pfarrprinzip", ZKT, 70 (1948),
pp. 169–98.

part of the social organization of the Church. Where several Christians pray together, where one helps another with good spiritual counsel, or comforts him in the power of the Holy Spirit, there truly Christian and so truly private life is at work. This is not just something that does happen in fact, but something which ought to happen. This is another thing which may never be replaced or repressed by official ecclesiastical organization, however necessary this too may be. There are, then, in the Church what we may call movements, "free groups" which extend into the social sphere but which do not stem from the Church's official organization, but are formed by individuals. There have always been charismatics without office in the Church to work at the care of souls, the prophets of the *Didache*, the monks with special graces in the ancient Greek Church, men like St. Benedict and St. Francis, who were not priests. Men like this have not the Church's authoritative mission to work upon other members of the Church; but when a man with such a gift lives a good Christian life and when other Christians feel the power of the Spirit in him and freely attach themselves to him, he should not have too many obstacles put in his way through unenlightened zeal or jealousy or a bureaucratic mania which cannot stand anything not to be officially organized. Otherwise we shall have an ecclesiastical totalitarianism which forgets that the

Church, too, is for men and not men for the Church, and that all official ecclesiastical organization and orders, even though they are necessary and have God's authority, are nevertheless subsidiary and may not stifle private religious community life, but must encourage it, protect and nourish it.

When we say that it is possible and right that lay charismatics should exist and work for souls in the Church, we are not saying anything against the ideal of the Latin Church, which does her uttermost to get charismatics with office or charismatic officials, or to put it more simply, holy priests. On the contrary, when official authority and personal charisma are united in one person (an occurrence which is very fortunate and desirable but cannot be brought about at will), when we have the holy official (it is obviously no accident that there is a special mass for confessor bishops, because such a fortunate occurrence must be celebrated in a special way), when a new pentecostal wind blows directly on the official Church, this is the best possible balance between office and spiritual gift, between the charismatic individual and the social organization of the Church.

One day the completed kingdom of God will come. Then there will be only individuals each with his own face and his own destiny which God's purely personal love has given to each one.

And these unique beings will be eternal because they were always more than just examples of the universal. But these individuals are loving individuals. And love is both unique and all-embracing. And so these unique beings form the communion of saints, the eternal kingdom of the love of God who is both One and All. And in it he is in everyone because he embraces all. For love unites by the very fact that it sets free and differentiates. Now we still have the Church militant. But in her the future age of liberating and uniting love is already at work. And because of this the visible Church gives the individual his freedom, and he achieves his free individuality in the Church by constantly and selflessly giving himself up to her service in humble and believing love.

## THE APPEAL TO CONSCIENCE

CONSCIENCE without any doubt belongs to the "eternal in man", to the things in him which are in a certain sense "absolute" and final. His theory of conscience, and, influenced by this, his conscience itself, depend in a peculiar way on the spiritual situation in which he hears its voice and judgement. This is what we are now going to consider. First we must examine certain current tendencies whose theory of the nature and function of conscience seeks to gain the acceptance of Catholics too; tendencies which take their origin from the general spiritual situation of our time and threaten the Christian doctrine of conscience. And, secondly, we must hold up against this theory the true Christian view. In our description of these tendencies we cannot here go into them fully, neither can we give evidence for them or the names of their propounders, nor can we discuss the question whether these tendencies exist or, where they actually exist, are as explicit and systematic as we make them here. It will be enough if we succeed in calling by their right name a few notions which are everywhere present as an anonymous danger.

*

The two tendencies which we want to describe here we could perhaps call extreme "situation-ethics" and the "mystique of sin". Let us try to understand their origin and nature:

## I. THE TENDENCY TOWARDS AN EXTREME SITUATION-ETHIC

We certainly are living in "extreme" times in moral matters as in others. That is to say the events and situations in which we must lead our moral life today make the morally right thing very often much more difficult than in former times both to know and to do. The enormously complex world-wide interdependence and development of economic and social life, the greater mental and spiritual differences between people, the constant threat to physical existence of hunger, war and economic catastrophe, the ever-present possibility of great encroachments into the private life of even the humblest and most unknown individual by state or party or economic forces, the over-population, the lack of accommodation, the subjection of all people to the influence of a quickly changing universally advertised "public opinion", the loosening or break-up of longstanding and stable bonds between the individual and his family, clan, home country, position in life and profession, the ease of travel which makes people nomads, the possibility that any opinion and any idea will be supported and campaigned for un-hindered, everywhere the overstrain on the emotions through the refinement of the entertainment industry, which offers people at any moment the ready-made possibility to escape from themselves —these, and many other things, make it extremely difficult today to know clearly and to do the morally right thing.

In former times life was simpler and more straightforward. The right way to behave was for the most part theoretically clear and easy to know, it had been tested and done before any number of times, and from a moral norm had become concretized in the code of behaviour of the society. Life then made the morally right behaviour also the most reasonable by the standards of utility, success and worldly profit, and the individual was to a large extent relieved of the responsibility of finding out and deciding what to do (at least in external actions).

What used to be an extreme borderline case in a moral situation which hardly ever occurred, has now become almost the "normal" case; there are very few things which everyone is agreed about; countless different and contradictory opinions are held about the right way to behave and each man has more or less to sift out the right one for himself; we know "statistically" how little the actual behaviour of people is in accordance with the officially held standards of behaviour; morally right behaviour leads only too easily to economic disadvantages which can even threaten existence; it has become dangerous to confess one's faith; the most normal marriage, even without bad will, only too often runs into the most serious moral difficulties; the unity and indissolubility of marriage are both threatened and family limitation is a very difficult problem; a political belief can sometimes be held only at the peril of one's life; today even the least intellectual of men who has already travelled about and seen foreign countries and other customs experiences the instability and changeability of the forms and norms of life today, and the bewildering extent to which the fundamental principles of religion and morality and behaviour in economic, social, sexual and political life are relative to time and place.

Perhaps we are also unconsciously influenced by a kind of "Protestant" dislike of a material moral norm in Christianity, by an unwillingness to accept that besides (or within) our trusting faith in God's forgiveness, other definite attitudes and actions can be of decisive importance to our salvation and justification in God's sight. Either expressly or involuntarily, our thought is extremely existentialist; where there is spirit, person and freedom, there is no "essence", no universal nature of man and his moral life, which can determine in advance, before he makes his free decision, the rightness or wrongness of his actions; hence there are no universal and universally binding norms, only the autonomous individual, who is in no way a "case" or "example" of the universal, and who alone can know in his own completely free choices how he must act and whether he has acted right. Today, much more easily and more often than in the "good old times", we are likely to feel that we are involved in theoretically insoluble dilemmas of conscience; the duty to confess our faith *and* the duty to care for the earthly wellbeing of our family; the duty not to kill the child in the womb *and* the duty to preserve the life of the mother; the duty not to commit adultery *and* the right, felt almost to be a duty, not to stunt one's own personal development; the duty to keep sexual life to marriage alone, *and* the assumed right to it even in circumstances where marriage may be impossible.

With such a situation combining all these possible difficulties become chronic and universal, we run the risk of a short circuit; we want to keep the moral law and obey the binding commands of our conscience, we—at least Christians—don't want to give in to a mere moral relativism and scepticism. But admittedly or unadmittedly, we give up hope of being able to clarify and master these overwhelmingly complex situations with definite, universally valid and justifiable—at least in general terms—moral norms. And so consciously or unconsciously, expressly in theory or implicitly in fact, we beat a retreat. We "detach ourselves from the enemy"—that is, we seek a solution which excludes in advance the actual case in which the dilemma occurs, and solves everything once and for all by holding that the difficulties experienced up till now present only apparent problems. We retreat to the "motive" for an action; we give up asking for definite ways of behaving, definite actions. *What* you do is not important, but only the motive for which you do it; if this is good nothing else matters before your conscience and before God. If, for example, we act in "love", then everything is all right, which, of course, implicitly or explicitly, presupposes that this love can realize itself in more or less any action, and so the action itself can be no criterion for whether it is really love. We retreat to "conscience"; we give up trying to clarify a difficult moral situation, to see it in the light of the universal and always universally binding norms of the natural law and the Christian revelation and thence to determine what is the one right thing, which God wills, to do here and now. We reduce Christianity's moral demands to perform definite actions to a purely formal duty to be faithful to our own conscience and brave enough to do what it tells us. We say (in the difficult and complex situations in which our conscience must make a decision): This is a case where everyone must go

4

by his own conscience; you must decide what to do yourself; the right thing to do, what your conscience tells you, depends entirely on the one concrete situation; it is a decision for one individual about one purely individual case. The norm for the individual conscience is no longer the objective nature of the act concerned, the moral law and the commandments of God, but in a sense, the conscience itself. The conscience is no longer the voice and the interpreter of a binding norm, about which an objective agreement among men is fundamentally possible, but, as it were, itself the lawgiver, which issues its decrees from which there is no appeal, unique and inscrutable, valid always for the one individual case alone.

There are different theories of how the conscience functions in such an extreme situation-ethic; in so far as people have a theory about their attitude at all, it may be an existentialist theory or a theory of unconditional loyalty to one's own freedom, or it may be more religious such as a kind of individual inspiration from above (even a pseudo-mysticism), but all these theories have this in common: The conscience is not the mediator of a law, but itself the source of moral decrees which are valid only once, only for me, only in this one situation; if they contradict the Church's teaching on the universal norms of the Christian moral law, this can no longer be adduced as a reason for calling these decrees in question. This kind of situation-ethic recognizes no moral norm which is universally binding, theoretically justifiable, and originates outside the conscience itself. In the eyes of its upholders, to dispute this extreme situation-ethic is a relapse into Old-Testament legalism, an exchange of outward forms for loving faith, a denial of the freedom of the children of God, an exaggerated essence-philosophy, which postulates a definite human nature unchanged throughout all the changing course of history, whereas in fact man is an undetermined existence free at every moment creatively to form himself anew. Quite a lot (not all!) of the dislike of moral-theological casuistry prevalent today among Catholics too is a symptom of an implicit situation-ethic of this kind: we should not and cannot try to clarify an individual case theoretically by referring it to general principles; the conscience can and must itself alone decide in the individual case what it thinks is right and what not. When a confessor, because it is too much trouble or because he is uncertain or afraid of a battle with his penitent, does not make the effort to clarify his penitent's dilemmas of conscience, which are certainly often very difficult and complex, and instead in almost every difficult case contents himself with saying: You must work this out with your own conscience, do what your conscience tells you; and when a Christian does not make the effort to confront himself and his actual behaviour with the moral law of the Church, when he will no longer recognize this teaching to be binding also on him in his situation, because he is afraid that this teaching could condemn his behaviour, when instead of this he explains that he has a good conscience, that he will take this on his own conscience, that in this case the Church is just speaking in general terms or too "theoretically", in this case she and her priests had no idea of the situation and could speak "lightly"—then we have a situation-ethic, perhaps unrecognized, at work.

## II. THE TENDENCY TOWARDS A MYSTIQUE OF SIN

A second danger to the Christian conscience today—if we may use a quick catchword to name what we mean—is a certain kind of mystique of sin. This attitude may generally be even more latent and unrealized, but there is no doubt that it is there. What we mean by mystique of sin is this: Only too often and too easily today in the complex and burdensome situations which he has to face, man experiences in himself and others guilt and moral failure, the collapse of his good will to know and to do the right thing. He knows (rightly) that even in this guilty situation God's mercy is still with him, calling him to repentance and to faith in the grace of the Redeemer; he knows that the Redeemer has come not to call the pharasaical self-righteous, but sinners who beat their breast and pray, Lord be merciful to me a sinner; he knows (rightly) that when we say we are not sinners we deceive ourselves and God's truth and love are not in us. And today much more than ever the true and earnest Christian feels that if God were to judge us according to his justice not one in a thousand could stand before him. It follows close upon this to think and to write and to act: We are sinners; we remain sinners; even when we have been justified we still can't keep God's commandments; but we are the real Christians just because we know that we are sinners and confess it and just because we do give God's mercy and overflowing grace the opportunity to manifest and fulfil itself; the important thing is not to avoid sin but trustingly to let ourselves be taken hold of by God's grace. Then comes the almost instinctive feeling that to do right and honestly strive to avoid sin is in the last resort pharasaical hypocrisy and self-righteousness, and the real and only possible way to be a good Christian is not to live a life of faithful observance of God's commandments, but to fall down at his feet in guilt and despair, as it is only when we are in this state of complete collapse that God can really be God to us: incomprehensibly merciful beyond all our deserts and all our hopes. When the Christian is described in modern Christian novels he is the guilty one whose life is broken and wrecked, and he no longer tries to do anything about it by beginning a new life and bringing forth fruits worthy of repentance and asking, "Brethren, what shall we *do*?" (Acts 2.37.) Instead he lets his earthly life hopelessly drain away and at the same time he is taken hold of by God's grace, which does not change him but takes hold of him and saves him unchanged, as it were, just from the outside. There is the danger that the commission of sins will come to be thought of as a necessary stage in a Christian life, without which the grace of God, which alone makes him a Christian and redeemed, could not exist at all. There is the danger already formulated by St. Paul: "Should we not continue in sin that grace may more abound?" (Rom. 6.1.) From this it is a short step, and logically follows, to teach, at least as a theory, a doctrine of universal salvation, which holds that each and all are in fact saved, and a short step to thinking that the most sublime and "supernatural" kind of co-operation in Christ's redemption is to share in the world's guilt by humbly becoming guilty with it. Briefly, there is the danger that the man who is in fact sinful and keeps on sinning, who is unstable and a moral wreck, might be idealized into *the* type and the only genuine type of the Christian, and that what is humanly sound and stable and firm, ordered and balanced, might be considered of no importance for actual Christian life. There is the danger that the only point at which the grace of God can take hold might be thought to be the point at which—from the human viewpoint —the man has broken down, the danger that grace might be seen only as forgiving and no longer as healing, redeeming and safeguarding, the danger, in a new form, of the gnostic heresy which holds that the God of the Redemption is not also the God of the Creation and its ordering, but that the earth and the flesh are essentially un-redeemable, and only when they prove themselves unredeemable to the very last, from above and remaining above, grace comes. This is what we mean by saying there is this danger which could wreck the true informing and right acting of our consciences, the danger of a morbid mystique of sin.

*

What should we now say about these two dangers? We shall try simply to hold up against them the Church's teaching. We do not mean to try and give the right answer to the concrete conscience-dilemmas which we used as examples to illustrate what we meant. The answers to these, which are indeed often difficult and in constant need of improvement, must be sought elsewhere. Here we give only basic principles which are necessarily only general.

### III. SITUATION-ETHICS

First of all, it goes without saying that a man must obey his conscience. For conscience is the most immediate giver of moral imperatives, and can never be passed over. Even if a conscience were objectively wrong about something, but in the concrete case the error could not be corrected, it would still have to be obeyed, because by its very nature it can never rightly be switched off or set aside or got round. Even in his obedience to his guiltlessly misinformed conscience, man is being obedient to God and paying homage to goodness. But it also goes without saying that the conscience is not automatically infallible; it can easily make mistakes and it is very difficult to distinguish *its* voice—the real voice of conscience —from the voice of precipitation, passion, convenience or self-will, or of a moral primitiveness which cannot see the finer distinctions or the more remote consequences of the act. And so man has a duty to do everything he can to conform his conscience to the objective moral law, to inform himself and let himself be taught and make himself prepared to accept (how difficult this often is!) instruction from the word of God, the magisterium of the Church and every just authority in its own sphere.

It is right that there should be a "conscience" which tells the individual man what he must do *as* an individual.[1] That is to say: that the individual is not just one member of the human race with a common human nature (he is this too), but also unique and irreplaceable, he has a sphere of moral choices which cannot be clearly decided by universal norms and laws alone, but need a special individual function of his conscience. Because the unique individual exists, there exists also an individual morality and a corresponding function of the conscience. But because the individual does not take away the universal, but by God's will lies within what is universally human in him, there is an individual morality only within a universal normative morality (but it *is* nevertheless there, although it is only too often overlooked); and there are individual moral imperatives only within the framework of universal Christian morality; and they can never go outside it.

It is right that the Christian conscience should be mature and of course this applies to the laity, and when it is not mature enough it should be told and encouraged to try and become so, in order to prevent society and the Church suffering severe damage. But this maturity of the Christian conscience is not an emancipation from and casting off of the universal norms preached by the Gospel and the Church by appealing to a unique situation and one's own conscience; it is the ability to apply these norms oneself to a concrete situation

Cf. Chapter 1, "The Individual in the Church", pp. 51 ff.

without needing help in every case, and the ability
to see moral duties and obligations also in cases
where the official universal norms are too abstract
and general to be applied by their official expo-
nents, either without great difficulty or at all.

But even though there is an individual morality
within the framework of universal morality, even
though maturity of conscience is an ideal to be
worked for, nevertheless there is no genuine
situation-ethic in the sense in which we described
it above.

First of all, it goes without saying for Catholics,
as was made clear at the time of the Reformation,
that morality is essential to a Christian and religious life. The fulfilment of the Commandments
is an essential part of Christianity as such, and not
just an indifferent matter, which is at most a field
for faith to manifest itself in (which is what a
"believing" situation-ethic logically leads to).

Furthermore, the Church teaches these commandments with divine authority exactly as she
teaches the other "truths of the Faith", either
through her "ordinary" magisterium or through
an act of her "extraordinary" magisterium in *ex
cathedra* definitions of the Pope or a general
council. But also through her *ordinary* magisterium, that is in the normal teaching of the Faith
to the faithful in schools, sermons and all the
other kinds of instruction. In the nature of the
case this will be the normal way in which moral

norms are taught, and definitions by Pope or general council the exception; but it is binding on the faithful in conscience just as the teaching through the extraordinary magisterium is. It is therefore quite untrue that only those moral norms for which there is a solemn definition (and these are criticised from all sides in the "world") are binding in faith on the Christian as revealed by God, and must be accepted by him as the rule for his own behaviour; and of course it is equally untrue—and this is often unadmittedly expected—that the moral law preached by the Church must necessarily receive the assent (even if it is only theoretical) of the non-Christian world. When the whole Church in her everyday teaching does in fact teach a moral rule everywhere in the world *as* a commandment of God, she is preserved from error by the assistance of the Holy Ghost, and this rule is therefore really the will of God and is binding on the faithful in conscience, even before it has been expressly confirmed by a solemn definition.

A moral norm is by nature universal but, precisely as a universal law, is intended to be the rule for the individual case. And so when it is fully grasped and rightly understood and interpreted (that is, understood as the magisterium means it, not just as an individual thinks fit to interpret it), and bears on an individual case, then this unique individual concrete case is bound by the norm and obliged to abide by it. When, for example, the Church teaches that *every* directly induced abortion is morally wrong, that every sacramentally contracted and consummated marriage between two baptized persons is indissoluble, then this applies to every individual case quite regardless of the circumstances. In these cases there is no "situation-ethic" by which, according to the circumstances (which of course everyone is tempted to regard as quite unique and extraordinary in his own case), the attempt is made to see if in this case the conscience—still "recognizing" the universal law, that is, for all other cases except this one—would not be objectively justified in considering another course of action right. A situation-ethic carried to its logical conclusion would become an ethical and metaphysical nominalism in which the universal could never actually bear upon the concrete with binding force. Of course, there will also often be the guiltlessly mistaken conscience which thinks, for special reasons in special circumstances, it may or must act differently from the moral norm which, without its knowing, is laid down by the Church. But, if it is not to degenerate into a merely private subjective voice, the Christian conscience has the duty to order itself by the objective moral norms. And if the Christian knows that these objective norms are to be found in the teaching of the Church, and if he knows that his case too (like every similar case) is meant by the law, then it is not easy to see how a believing Christian can still logically and guiltlessly come to the conclusion that in his situation the "case" is morally other than the universal law judges it to be. If in such cases he would at least admit that from human weakness he had offended against the law, which he was nevertheless bound to keep, then it would be easier to help him. But those who think that in their individual case they can still objectively justify their offence against the law by appealing to their situation with subtle theoretical excuses, or by appealing to their "conscience", or even to a private enlightenment from God, are in very serious and dangerous error. They can only succeed in deceiving themselves, for they are suppressing God's truth.

When a man has once realized (and in this age of psychoanalysis one would expect this realization to be widespread; unfortunately it isn't) how easily and in what refined ways he can deceive himself, how quickly what is desired by him appears also justified to him, how hidden and distorted the final standards are by which he in fact judges and values things, how "obvious" something can seem to us when it is in fact a very dubious and problematic case, then he will be more careful in his appeals to a "good conscience". And anyone who has read the first chapter of St. Paul's Epistle to the Romans has read how God judges the doubtless very "respectable" Jews and Gentiles (and where are there *no* people who think themselves very respectable?); and he will have been dismayed to find that the "good conscience" of respectable people who know at once what God asks of them and what he "naturally" can't expect of us, is only too often just the punishment and result of their blind but still responsible sinfulness: their real conscience has been muted leaving their heart to say what it will unhindered, and the Scripture says the heart of man is evil from his youth. If we Christians, when faced with a moral decision, really realized that the world is under the Cross on which God himself hung nailed and pierced, that obedience to God's law can also entail man's death, that we may not do evil in order that good may come of it, that it is an error and heresy of this eudemonic modern age to hold that the morally right thing can never lead to a tragic situation from which in this world there is no way out; if we really realized that as Christians we must expect almost to take for granted that at some time in our life our Christianity will involve us in a situation in which we must either sacrifice everything or lose our soul, that we cannot expect always to avoid a "heroic" situation, then there would indeed be fewer Christians who think that their situation requires a special ruling which is not so harsh as the laws proclaimed as God's laws by the Church, then there would be fewer confessors and spiritual advisers who, for fear of telling their penitent how strict is God's law, fail in their duty and tell him instead to follow his conscience, as if he had not asked, and done right to ask, *which* among all the many voices clamouring within him was the true voice of God, as if it were not for God's Church to try and distinguish it in accordance with his law, as if the true conscience could speak even when it had not been informed by God and the faith which comes from hearing.

A man who has learnt—by the grace of God!—to beware of man because he is a liar (*omnis homo mendax*) and so beware of himself because he is a man, will no longer be able to say so lightly: I will make this right with my conscience; what the priests say is just red tape. Must we make the thing right "with our conscience" or in fact—putting it more exactly and more honestly—with God? And doesn't God speak most clearly—precisely in complicated and difficult cases—by his own word through the mouth of his Church?—so we can only be certain that we are really hearing the voice of our conscience and not the voice of our own sinful inclinations when this voice agrees with the Church's teaching. The priests are not erecting red tape when they abide by the teaching of the Church, but they are telling us the word of God. Is it really extraordinary that this word (which is God's) is so "unrealistic" and so "unsuited to the times", when "reality" is against God and the times are evil and the Christian must be prepared to take his stand for God against "reality" and the "times" even unto death?

But if this is the case, what has become of the freedom of the children of God? Does this not put us back under the rule of the letter which kills and is only the law of sin? (Cf. 1 Cor. 15.56.) Isn't it true that we may "love and do what we will"? It is true that where the Spirit of the Lord, who justifies, teaches and gives us divine life, moves a man, then he is no longer *under* the law, he is free from the law, the letter of which is imposed on him with binding force and reveals in him the helplessness of a man weakened and enslaved by sin; when the Spirit is strong and powerful within a man and binds him immediately to God above all law in a relationship of fully personal love, then the law is "superseded" by the inner law of the heart, the law of Christ in the power of which we not only know within us what is right but can have the strength freely to do it. But in order to be free like this we must really have the Spirit; this Spirit can be lost; and man the liar can deceive himself that he has this Spirit when he really hasn't. We have not got the Spirit if we do not keep God's laws, and we can only keep these laws in the Holy Spirit in whom

God's will and God's power are one, and in whom alone we can have true Christian freedom. He who boasts of the freedom of the children of God, when asked, Do we then overthrow the law? must answer with St. Paul: By no means, on the contrary we uphold the law. (Rom. 3.31.) He must know and live the Scripture; he who fulfils the law shall live (Gal. 3.12); the *doers* of the law will be justified before God. (Rom. 2.13.) The law has come to an end because it has been superseded, not by the arbitrary choices of our human will but by the power of the Holy Spirit. But the only way of knowing whether we have the Holy Spirit in us is precisely by whether we fulfil the law. And even the sinner, who flies to Christ's grace and finds therein salvation and justification, only really flies to Christ in his conversion if he confesses that he has become guilty precisely because the grace, which would have given the power to want and to do the will of God, has through his own fault remained ineffective, only really flies to Christ if he is truly prepared not only to seek forgiveness from God for the things he has left undone, but to do God's will henceforth; for "if any man says that God's commandments cannot be fulfilled even by those who have been justified and given grace, let him be anathema". (Council of Trent, sess. 6, can. 18.)

To the free children of God also it is said (in
5

the eternal freedom of God it will no longer need
to be said; but now it must still be said because
they are in danger of confusing their true freedom
with the desires of their flesh): Do not deceive
yourselves, neither the debauched, nor idolaters,
nor adulterers, nor sodomites, nor thieves, nor
misers, nor drunkards, nor revilers, nor extor-
tioners will inherit the kingdom of God. (1 Cor.
6.9.) We can do "everything" only when we love.
But we are not loving if we do evil. Are there not
today many "good" Christians who subtly and
dishonestly try and make the freedom of Christians a justification for a pact between right living
and godlessness, light and darkness, Christ and
Belial in their moral life, who do everything they
want, good or evil, and then say they still love,
instead of really loving (which calls for the
greatest renunciation) and then doing everything
which a man who really loves God may do?

And so it remains: The commandments of God
come truly and plainly out of the mouth of the
Church and they require obedience whether in
this or that case they are easy to apply or not;
they are the will of the living God who has spoken
to us through Jesus Christ our Lord—the will of
God—which is also for his children who are
justified and living in grace and the freedom of
the Holy Spirit. The Faith which justifies before
God is the loving Faith which does God's will.

## IV. THE MYSTIQUE OF SIN

We must now say a little more about that tendency which we called a mystique of sin.

First of all, it goes without saying for Christians that Christianity is salvation also for those who have fallen into sin before God, because without the grace which preserves from sin or saves from sin no man could be sinless in God's sight. Whenever a man, from the depths of his sin, looks up to God in faith and repentance and grace, and longs for him and accepts his gift of salvation in Christ Jesus, there is more joy in heaven over this one sinner than over ninety-nine just men who think they need no repentance. It goes without saying that salvation is nearer to the broken— even if it is their own sins they are broken by —and humble in heart than to the self-righteous, with their miserable respectability which is often only a deceptive façade to cover their inner rottenness. It goes without saying that God's grace has secret ways which we cannot fathom, which are not our ways, of redeeming and saving men who in human eyes can only seem far from God. His grace is beyond our understanding and does not have to give an account of itself to us. He binds us, not himself, to the ways which he has shown us.

But it is true as well that he who honestly says,
I have sinned, must also say, I will arise and go
to my Father. But in God's country there is no
commerce between light and darkness, God and
sin. It is a defined truth of the Faith that God's
grace makes it possible for the man who has been
justified to keep God's commandments, so that if
he falls again into sin, he falls although he could
have stood firm and he himself is the really
responsible, guilty cause of this fall. And so a
conscience which tries to comfort the sinner with
the thought that he could not avoid sinning, and
that this sin was in fact no danger to his salvation,
as long as even in his sin he went on trusting in
God's forgiveness, is not the voice of grace, but
the voice of the man's own self-delusion, which
wants an easy compromise between sin and God.
"Felix culpa" can only be said by those who
through God's grace have overcome sin. That
God writes straight on crooked lines gives the
creature no right to draw crooked lines in his
book of life. Such an act which actually plans and
calculates to make sin a stage in his development
is a creature's most hateful *hubris*, which is prepared to outwit God's mercy, which tries to see
and calculate human life from God's standpoint,
and is arrogance and self-delusion of such a
serious nature that God threatens to answer it not
with his grace but with his justice. Precisely because sin can be committed not only immediately

and expressly in the sphere of faith and trust, but also in the moral sphere in the narrower sense, in the sphere of the Commandments, and because from the creature's point of view there is no way of getting rid of it, no way out, man never has the right to surrender himself "in faith" into this position merely because he imagines he can still hope for forgiveness and that even while he sins God's grace will not abandon him. If God gives his grace to a man who *has* sinned, this is always a new action of God's grace which is in no way due to the man, and cannot be calculatingly relied on before the sin is committed. It is curious how these upholders of an existentialist mystique of sin all of a sudden fall into an essentialist philosophy, which is quite out of place here and makes the unpredictable miracle of God's forgiving grace suddenly become an essential of man's existence which is always at his disposal and can be counted on in advance.

When—particularly in modern Catholic novels —we hear described for us how grace seeks and finds even him who was lost, we read this gratefully as an echo of the Gospel. But at the same time we must guard ourselves against misunderstanding this echo, as if all Christian existence was contained in this kind of deliverance alone. On the contrary, it is always something more; it is a new life (even when the only thing that has to be done in this new life is to endure a miserable

ending to our earthly life), it is the sanctification
of the world, it is work in faith and grace, it is
bearing fruit in the Holy Ghost, it is the ever-
renewed striving (even when in fact it breaks
down again and again) to bring about the reign of
the kingdom of God in ourselves and the world.
Whatever is healthy or morally fine or well
ordered and harmonious, even apparently on the
purely human level, is (even when this is not
realized) a manifestation of grace and the divine
life which is entrusted to us and demanded of us,
because the Word became flesh not to save us
*from* the flesh because it had been corrupted by
sin, but to save the flesh *itself*. It does not make
this salvation any the less God's action that it also
comes about, and must do, through our action, for
our action is already his grace.

We are today all threatened by the danger of
cultural, spiritual and moral collapse. But even if
this comes upon us, we shall let God be greater
than our collapse and even in our fall grasp his
saving grace in faith. But we shall not sinfully and
morbidly make this possible collapse the corner-
stone of a system in advance, as if it were the only
genuine Christian situation. If we have a break-
down of this kind we shall only still be able to
attain salvation and blessing through it if we fight
against it. And so—not in naive worldly optimism
but in obedience to our Christian mission and in
courage and hope through the grace of God—

even at this late hour in the history of our Western civilization, we love what is wholesome and hopeful and good and make it the goal of our striving which *we* must try and attain, whatever God may do with us, for what he does is for him and not us to decide. A man with this attitude praises the power and glory of grace better than one who is obsessed by his possible moral collapse and thinks he can only survive it by regarding it merely as a scheme of victorious grace. The true praise of *sola gratia* does not need the help of a mystique of sin.

# 3

## A NEW FORM OF HERESY

___

S T. PAUL says that schisms—heresies—must come. Whatever St. Paul himself may have meant by "heresy", in the history of the Church the word has always been taken to mean what we mean by it today; the distortion of the word of God preached by the Church into a human error, by a Christian who makes his own fancy and his own standard a measure of the word of God, and suits it to himself instead of himself to it, and so sets up his own Christianity against the Church's. That they "must" come is the natural consequence of the freedom of fallen man, and results from sin or error or both. But *that* this heresy comes and will come—although God's greater power and grace never abandons us—is for the Christian who has been instructed by God's prophetic word not just a chance surprise which one may expect soon to disappear because it should not have happened at all, but is something the Christian already knows about—heresy, like sin and guilt and stress and despair, will accompany human life and the history of the kingdom of God till the end of the world. And so there "must" be heresies, because they are more than just the consequences of a misused freedom; they belong to those mysterious things which "must" be so that no man, and so no man's truth either, can boast before God.

And therefore the Christian will not be surprised when he encounters heresies. He will even expect them and regard them as an inevitable and even as the greatest and highest, and so "necessary", temptation, in which darkness really clothes itself in the garments of light. And when the Christian encounters no heresy, none which could really tempt in this way as a real challenge, he will not consider his peace of spirit something to be taken for granted, but will ask himself in dismay whether perhaps the eyes of his spirit have become so blind and his heart so insensitive to the difference between truth and falsehood that he can no longer recognize a heresy when he meets one; whether the age and country he lives in no longer produce heresies because at bottom, in spite of their formal acceptance of all the truths of the Faith, they have become so indifferent to God's truth that they no longer need to mitigate the remorselessness of revelation by setting up human systems in its stead.

If, then, there must be heresies, today too and "specially for me", where, then, are the heresies which we must guard against? What form will they take today in order to deceive people the more easily? One might think that this ques-

tion was quickly answered! The world in which
Christians live like a flock of scattered and
hunted sheep, is full of errors which contradict
the Word of God which has come to us in Christ
Jesus; this error proclaims itself loudly and
with conviction from all the newspapers, shouts
out of loudspeakers, dresses up in the works of
the poets, and is at work in the business of the
world which—as always—is inclined to evil; it is
the spiritual atmosphere in which we must live
and breathe, day in, day out. In these days a
Christian has not far to look for heresies, if he is
seeking them because they "must" be. This answer
is right. But it does not describe the whole situation of the Christian in the face of heresy today.
For the errors which this answer has in mind no
longer claim to be *Christian* truth, a genuine
interpretation of the revelation entrusted by God
to the Church. They call themselves, openly and
honestly, unchristian, and don't set any store by
being regarded as the Church's truth. So the
Christian who listens to the Church's teaching
can make light work of them. True that in his
practical life and everyday dealings he will very
often live more in accordance with the spirit of
the world than the truth of the Church. But nevertheless, if he seeks the truth his spirit is to accept,
the principles by which he is to live, he will have
little difficulty in distinguishing the errors of the
world, which do not pretend to be Christian, from

the message of the Gospel. It has never been—at least so it seems—so easy as it is today to draw the necessary fine distinction between what is world and what is Christianity, so long, of course, as one really and unquestionably wants to be a Christian at all. For, as we said, the world of the spirit today no longer always claims to represent only the message of the Gospel, and it has never been so easy to know clearly what Christ and his Church's teaching is as it is in this our modern age when the Church (above all in the First Vatican Council) has developed her understanding of herself to the point of formulating precisely and finally the nature of her teaching authority and the way in which it functions.

And so the errors meant by the answer which we criticized are in fact not heresies, not Christian errors. They are clearly "outside". They can no longer tempt us by claiming to be the true Christian faith. They can indeed be a temptation—and naturally a very strong one—to the Christian to leave the Church and Christian truth, and base his spiritual life on something else. But to regard and defend these errors as Christian and Catholic truth is no longer possible for Catholics as it was in former times. This means (to put the same thing in yet another way) that heresy in the form it used to take, which we still wrongly take for granted is the only form for any heresy, is no longer so dangerous a temptation to the Christian as it used to be. Of course, in former centuries too the Christian had to know that Christ's gospel had been entrusted to his Church, and that *she* is the guardian and authoritative exponent of God's word.

But where and how this Church speaks, and where and how to find out what she says, was not so clear then as now. For example, during the Arian controversy, would it have been possible for every Catholic (as it would be today) to tell by a clear, easily accessible principle which was universally recognized beforehand as revealed, *where* the Church was actually speaking? Even today theologians have difficulty in establishing that a council was ecumenical except by the assent of the Pope to it—that is, by the help of a principle which in earlier times was indeed objectively present and in action, but which had not then been expressly and precisely formulated, and so did not belong to the universally recognized dogmas of the Faith. And so it happened that on the one hand the true Faith and heresy could both claim to be Christ's Church, and on the other hand, the Christian did not have as an indisputable Christian truth the formal principle by which to distinguish between these claims. Today it is different. The magisterium of the Church is not only (as it objectively always was) present with binding force in the word of the Bishop of Rome, but this fact is itself a truth of the Faith which must be accepted in advance by the Catholic Christian; but this was not so clear in earlier ages. Because today the formal principle of faith has itself become part of the body of doctrine which the Catholic must believe, his position is different from that of a Christian in former times; if in any question under discussion he sets his own opinion up against that of a papal definition, in doing so he would know that he was setting himself up against a truth of the Faith, which *he himself* had already acknowledged as his own faith—that is, that not only the true Church as a whole (whose voice it is not always easy to distinguish) but also the Roman See is the final judge of what is and what is not the true meaning of revelation. By the very act of holding this opinion which was against the principle he himself had acknowledged up till then, this Catholic would be putting himself outside the Church, which up till then he had acknowledged as the only true Church of Christ, and he himself could know clearly that he was doing this. And so today it is not possible to advocate an erroneous doctrinal opinion *in the Church* which one has acknowledged, in accordance with the formal definitions, to be the only true Church of Christ.

Is there then no more heresy *in* the Church? Is heresy now only possible outside the Church, because on the one hand the true Church, as guardian of the truth, points out heresies as soon as they arise, and on the other hand, the Catholic knows clearly in advance *where* the Church is and where she speaks, without a general council or some other means of discovering the universal consensus of bishops being necessary to establish or support it? Or are there still heresies *in* the Church today because they "must" be, and so must be in the Church, because being threatened and assaulted by heresy is a necessary element of Christian existence in the world?

Let us accept for the moment—if only as a working hypothesis—that there "must" also be heresy *in* the Church. Then because of what we have said, it is clear in advance that this heresy will have to assume a different form from that of previous heresies. In former times heresy existed undisguised and open, even *in* the Church (by "Church" meaning, of course, not her objective essence in its reality, but the actual group of people whom the men of those days could have thought of as this reality), because the formal principle of faith had not become expressly and bindingly part of the content of faith by which the boundaries of the Church could be clearly defined. Today, on the other hand, an *open* heresy (that is, one which is clearly and precisely formulated) held by a Catholic is shown to be against the teaching of the Church immediately the Pope condemns it, and this by principles which the Catholic himself has already expressly owned and acknowledged; he must either give up the heresy or leave the Church, which would be to deny a doctrine which up till then he had expressly acknowledged as a truth of his own faith. If in spite of this there is still heresy *in* the Church today, it can no longer be open but must have become covert and hidden. It must (if it exists) have become a sort of cryptogam. If it is not to die out, the disease of heresy cannot be plainly visible, and easy to diagnose from its formulated teaching in opposition to the teaching of the Church; but it must now be a hidden, nameless sickliness which saps the spiritual life-force, a "creeping" sickness.

If we take our *a-priori* hypothesis a little further and ask what, more precisely, will this hidden heresy be like (if it exists), we must consider again the reason why it can no longer come out in the open. The reason is that open heresy would immediately come up against the Church's magisterium in the form which, unlike a general council, is always there in readiness to react quickly and clearly to the whole Church—the teaching authority of the Pope—and the fact of this authority has already been acknowledged as part of his faith by the would-be heretic. The heresy would have to be hidden and covert, cryptogamic, so that in practice it would be more or less impossible for the papal magisterium to get at it. But this magisterium can only pronounce judgement on a heresy if it is openly formulated in clear intellectual terms above the level of mere feeling and attitude. If the heresy is not thus formulated, the magisterium clutches at air, for this is the only kind it can cope with. And hence this latent heresy has two principal methods: on the one hand it avoids coming into conflict with the magisterium by avoiding clear statements in books, official teaching etc., and taking refuge in the private and esoteric domain reserved for the initiated only; on the other hand, it keeps to the vague and approximate, the undefined attitude, and in writing concerns itself only with the doubtful, with "attempts", and with the exposition of unsolved problems (but in fact meaning more than this), passing over truths which contradict it in silence. To put it more briefly: Heresy in the Church today (if it exists) must and can take cover, and by being indifferent in theory and in fact to the truths of the Faith which contradict it, can remain latent in the Church.

Before we now go on to ask whether this new[1] form of heresy, which we have built up *a priori*,

---

[1] Of course only relatively "new". We don't deny that there could have been fairly similar phenomena for different reasons earlier in the Church's history. We only mean that this form of heresy is "typical" today, for the reasons we have given here.

really exists in the Church, we must first say a little more about it in order to avoid misunderstandings. When we speak of the methods employed by heresy in the Church we must *not* think only or first and foremost of conscious heresy, which its advocate incurs guilt in holding. Of course *contumacia* belongs to the Church's *legal* concept of heresy, because only thus can it be guilty and matter for the Church's right to punish. But this is not the point for us at the moment. For in the sense we mean here every error which in fact is contradictory to God's revelation, every distorted notion and every false interpretation of the Faith, which stems from an unchristian mental attitude, is heresy and a man who in the daily course of his life does not live by the truth, and does not even reckon with it—as friend or enemy —in his behaviour, is a heretic. At least it is material heresy and we should notice that in our case this material heresy is not formulated, but is expressed in a way of behaving, an attitude, a vague and general feeling which can permeate all a man's thought and behaviour. And here we should observe that heresy is not only dangerous to salvation in so far as it is disobedience of the will, but independently of this question of guilt in the will, it is also dangerous in so far as it is a lack of truth and reality in the understanding. Because the man who is in error is missing the truth which means salvation to him, his error is dangerous whether he holds it in good will or in bad.[1] It is also not true that a heresy in the sense we mean could not exist in a man together with an earnest will to believe right. For the mind of man contains and lives by far more than what it consciously adverts to, and can be moved at the same time by different "spirits".

And it is not true that this heresy can only exist in the men of the *hearing* Church. It can exist in all the members of the Church. If we are all sinners and are all affected in some measure by self-opinion, arrogance, spiritual sloth and indifference which (beginning in our will) spreads to our understanding and to what we teach with it, then it is only to be expected that this vague heresy can exist also in the members of the *teaching* Church. Of course the Spirit of truth,

[1] The modern Christian has almost completely ceased to realize the danger to salvation of error in belief. He thinks of error in matters of faith as a threat to salvation only as the expression of the bad will of the man who holds it; it is not knowledge of the truth as such which is important, but the moral disposition. If the ancient Christian conviction that error is dangerous to salvation (whether the will is good or bad) is right, and nevertheless there can be guiltless error which does not destroy salvation, it is only possible to reconcile the two by saying that even in and with this error a man can still attain, according to his knowledge, what is necessary of the reality upon which salvation depends; and vice versa, if he cannot do this, then there must be guilt, and it is not possible that every (existential) error could be guiltless.

who has been promised to the Church, will guard
the holders of the magisterium from ever solemnly
defining an error to be of faith. And it is also
certain that over and above this the help of the
Spirit is at the disposal of the Church's official
teachers in full measure. But when there is
narrowness of spirit, self-will and obstinacy, when
people go in for hair-splitting and rivalries between schools—and this is also possible in the
teaching Church—truth and understanding, and
so the teaching of it, cannot be as it should be.
There are distortions and narrowings which one
can go on thinking for a long time are an integral
part of truth as it is revealed, believed and taught.
This existential "colouring" of the truths taught
(if we may so put it) can in some way reflect the
sinful individuality of the holders of the magisterium, even if nothing positively false is taught.
Because of the hardness of heart and indifference
of the Church's teachers the truth of the Gospel
can be preached in a way which makes the men
who hear the teaching at that time unable to grasp
it sufficiently and really make it their own. Who
could deny *a priori* that there have been times
(and perhaps there still are) when, at least by way
of failure to realize the living import of the truth,
there has been error in the teaching Church and
in this sense "heresies"? Could anyone deny (if he
believes in the "Church of sinners") that the light

of the Gospel too, not only the love, has not always and at all times shone so brightly in the earthly lamp of the Church as God would have it shine? If we now ask whether the hidden heresy we have been considering *a priori* actually exists in the Church today, and exists more prevalently than in former times (because then heresy could more easily remain in the Church, at least for a time, in open form), we mean heresy in the widest sense, to cover all the forms of spiritual unawareness which are the sign or the result of a man not holding onto God's truth with all his heart and strength.

We have postulated these hidden heresies, in the widest sense, *a priori*; heresies must be and must be in the Church because she is a Church of sinful men. But do they in fact exist in the Church? We think they do. In the encyclical *Spiritus Paraclitus* Benedict XV says there are people, even teachers of the sacred sciences, who attack in secret some of the teachings of the Church. (*DB*, 2186.) This "occulta oppugnatio" which Benedict XV says does happen in the Church of our time, is the most enormous form of the hidden heresy we are referring to. And there is no doubt that it is not yet dead. Think, for example, of the books published by Mensching and Mulert before the last war, advocating a "Reformed Catholicism"; they did, of course, contain open heresies (open, that is, if we don't count the anonymity of the authors), and so could be condemned as heretical by the Church, but these heresies were the reflection of an attitude and a teaching which could be called covertly heretical, because the authors, while admitting that their theories were against the Church's teaching, nevertheless did not want to be expelled from the Church and so chose to remain anonymous.[1]

But the most enormous kind of hidden heresy, which clearly took shape for the first time in the history of modernism, is not the only kind or the most important or the most dangerous. Much more frequent (although difficult to pin down) is an attitude of mistrust and resentment against the Church's magisterium, a widespread feeling of

---

[1] It is beyond the scope of this essay to answer the question why Christians who know that their theories are against the Church's official teaching nevertheless want to stay in the Church. Besides the reason we have already mentioned—that by leaving the Church they would also be contradicting a defined truth about the Church and her magisterium—there are other reasons too; a man of today is no longer as ready to trust his own opinion as he was in the times of self-conscious individualism and liberalism; he is no longer so convinced of it that he could easily set up a religious community himself, without getting lost in sectarianism and enthusiasm etc. When people have this feeling and yet cannot bring themselves to believe unconditionally in the Church then we get—since the time of modernism— the attempt to build a private little chapel within the big Church, an esoteric sect within the big community.

being suspiciously and narrowly controlled by it
in research and teaching, the feeling that "one
can't say what one thinks" (but one is nevertheless
justified in thinking it in "good" conscience).
Doesn't one come across the feeling that one can
say more (at least among friends) than one can
write? Or the attitude that one should be glad that
this and that has been said by Protestant theologians outside the Church, and one has to go to
them to read it because one could not say it
without risk oneself? One sometimes gets the
impression that the theoretical opinions of a
theologian are hidden under the form of his historical research to make them more acceptable
because less evident. Isn't there here and there
something like an esoteric teaching which is only
spread by word of mouth? Isn't there unformu-
lated heresy which avoids clear exposition in print
and works by omissions and one-sided perspec-
tives, overstepping explanation and going straight
from the wrong attitude to wrong practice? How
often, for example, do people purposely avoid
mentioning hell, or pass over in silence, or with at
most a few uncertain and embarrassed mumblings
if it can't be avoided, the evangelical counsels,
consecrated virginity and the celibacy of the
clergy? How often does the preacher preach to
the educated people in his congregation about
temporal punishment for sin, indulgences, angels,

fasting, the devil (at most he will talk about "the demonic" in man), purgatory, prayer for the Holy Soula and other old-fashioned things? When "inner freedom" is recommended "to develop positively in the Church and to treat the confessional in its present state as incompetent so long as it exercises the sacrament of forgiveness in the service of sex-molochism",[1] then the practice of this hidden heresy has found its formal theory, namely the express recommendation to live heresy in secret.

But there is yet another form of this hidden heresy, and, paradoxically, it can affect those who are proudest of their longstanding and unimpeachable orthodoxy; heresy in the form of indifference. God's truth is always one and the same and final; it is preached by the Church's magisterium. When this magisterium has defined the truth entrusted to her by Christ in a form which is binding in conscience on the Christian, then this truth is true and valid in this form for all time; the Church's preaching and theology will always refer back to these formulations of the truth made in the course of the Church's history in the sure knowledge that in them the truth concerned really is rightly expressed (although, of course, any formulation of a truth of the Faith, because it is in human words, can never express it adequately, and at least in principle, could be replaced by a still better and

[1] Ernst Michel, *Die Ehe*, Stuttgart, 1949, p. 128.

fuller formula); a formulation in intellectual concepts is never just an attempt to put into words an experience of the Faith which is in itself non-rational (as in the modernist misconception of the intellectual element in the Faith). But this truth of God in human words is not meant merely to go on being monotonously repeated in stereotyped phrases in theology textbooks. It is meant to come into living contact with the individual Christian, to take on flesh and blood, penetrate his heart and mind and bring him the truth. Each man anew has to make it his own. Each man, with his own experiences, his own vocation and his whole spiritual situation, which is not only that of Catholic Christianity but the general spiritual situation of his time, must individually hear God's message anew. And because a man's faith is not the message that could be heard but the message he *does* hear, and because the truth of revelation cannot exist on earth in one eternally static and valid form but only as it is actually believed by men, the plain unchanging truth of the Gospel, as it is actually heard and understood by men of every age, must bear the mark of that age upon it. If it doesn't, or doesn't sufficiently, this does not make it timeless and universally valid; it is much more likely to mean that it wears the garb of another age, which men have become used to, and because it is ancient and customary have falsely come to think of it as *the* expression of the eternally unchanging truth of the Gospel. This freezing of the form in which the truth of the Gospel is expressed is in fact a dangerous symptom of indifference, whether conscious or not, to the truth, the symptom of a lack of power to assimilate it existentially and express it in new terms. Who could doubt that this form of heresy also exists in our time—heresy in which dead orthodoxy is only the expression and the result of a secret indifference to the truth, in which a thing is left unchanged because men are so indifferent that they do not want to have to go to the trouble of getting rid of it or questioning it?

If anyone thinks that all this has been said so that we should now go about smelling heresies everywhere and ferreting them out, he has not understood the point. We only referred to the signs of the actual existence of this hidden heresy by way of *a-posteriori* support for the *a-priori* thesis that today there must be this changed form of heresy. Anyone who wants to draw practical consequences from this theological speculation should first of all look to himself. For the kind of heresy we mean here cannot be guarded against merely by the good will to believe rightly and be obedient to the Church's magisterium.

From all this it follows naturally that the usual methods of dealing with heresy up till now are of relatively little use against this latent kind. The Church can preach the truth, she can herself conceptually formulate heretical tendencies (as Pius X did for the first time in his encyclical against modernism) and then refute them in this form. But she can do little against mute heresy, she is for the most part helpless against heresy which only speaks in correct statements and keeps silent on those which do not suit it, against the heresy of indifference and a theologically sterile integralism. She is inevitably tempted today to make the difficulty even greater. And for the same reason as that which has caused this changed form of heresy. Because (since the First Vatican Council) the magisterium of the Church knows that it is itself an object of faith it is more likely now than in former times to be tempted to suppress heretical opinions with its formal authority alone, without ensuring that they are pulled up by the roots. There is the temptation to fight heresy only by *administrative* measures (by putting books on the Index, removing suspect teachers etc.) instead of by actual *magisterial* measures (by positively formulating the true doctrine so that the error is really uprooted); the temptation to impose silence without also speaking out the truth or allowing someone else to, and speaking it out in a way which is not only true but which can penetrate mind and heart. The temptation is not insuperable, as we said, but it is present (that is not to say, given in to), and belongs in the situation of this changed form of heresy, because it is caused by the same thing. Wasn't there, for example, too long a silence over many questions of biblical theology in the time of modernism?

At any rate, today there is unavoidably a greater danger than ever before that by officially suppressing hasty unripe theological theses and opinions heresy will not be killed but only changed into its new form, which will really enable it to resist the measures of the magisterium against it. For, so it seems to us, the development of the Church and the knowledge of her formal teaching authority as itself an object of faith "must" bring with it a form of heresy which, in this context, has not existed up till now.

"If they (the clergy) do not allow the people to speak their minds, do not, in more dignified language, encourage or even tolerate, with courage and forbearance and even a certain optimism free from anxiety, the growth of a public opinion within the Church, they run the risk of directing her from a soundproof ivory tower, instead of straining their ears to catch the voice of God, which can also be audible within the clamour of the times."

*from*

# FREE SPEECH IN THE CHURCH

*also by* FR. RAHNER

4/- net

The author is concerned in this book with the function, scope and limitations of public opinion in the Church. He maintains that one of the most important duties of Christians is that of discussion and criticism, indispensable in any mature society. Against the Church's growing freedom from the dubious social privileges of the past, Dr. Rahner sets the picture of a Church member stronger than ever in loyalty through the development of a truly adult capacity for comment, discussion and personal initiative. And it is with reference to this lively conception of the individual Catholic that he boldly discusses in his second essay the prospects of Christianity today.

# THE STUDY OF THEOLOGY

## CHARLES DAVIS

30/-

"This is a work of really splendid and exciting scope. It should prove thrilling to the theologian and will make no greater demands on the layman than a serious book on any specialised subject. There is little or no technical language, but with exactness and economy of words the new concepts, not yet captured in text book phrases, are expressed in clear English. It is just the mingling of the warmer streams of contemporary biblical, liturgical and catechetical thinking with the familiar currents of speculative theology that gives the wonderful wholeness and balance which make the Christian themes here presented so heartening."

*Irish Independent*

### also by FR. DAVIS

# LITURGY AND DOCTRINE

4/6

"One of the most refreshing books I have read in years. It is both short and cheap. There is no member of the English Catholic community who would not benefit from buying it and reading it."

Laurence Bright, O.P., in *The Life of the Spirit*

"One hopes that *Liturgy and Doctrine* will enjoy a very wide circulation . . . I wish it could be made compulsory reading, not only for Catholics but for non-Catholics too." *Eastern Churches Quarterly*

# TO KNOW CHRIST JESUS

F. J. SHEED                    Paper 10/6, Cloth 21/-

"When Dr. Sheed wrote *Theology and Sanity* it seemed unlikely that he could ever produce a work to match it. It was so unusual to see a layman moving in on the territory of professional theologians, distilling the fruits of their labours into a manageable volume and giving to English-speaking Catholics an invaluable statement of what their faith should mean to them. He *has* done it again. This time he has spoiled the Scripture scholars and produced a work which cannot fail to achieve a success even greater than that of the previous book. After all, theology remains something of an acquired taste, even when presented as Dr. Sheed presents it. This time a much wider audience awaits him. Few Christians who can read at all will fail to find this an enthralling book. He has written what must surely be one of the most satisfying studies of the Gospels ever made.
. . . " if you think you have no more to learn about the Gospels, **this is your book**; if you find the Gospels boring, **this is your book**; if you find them incomprehensible, meaningless, too deep, too obvious, **this is your book.** If you should know anybody who has never even opened the Gospels, you cannot do better than give him this book."

Rev. Thomas Corbishley in *The Month*

". . . F. J. Sheed illuminates familiar material by placing it in a fresh context of theological understanding." *The Spectator*

"Mr. F. J. Sheed has become widely known as one of the leading lay theologians among Roman Catholics, and has enriched the literature of devotion and learning with many books that add beauty to integrity. His latest book is a pilgrimage through the Gospels, with comment on what we find there." *British Weekly*

# THE RESURRECTION

## F. X. DURRWELL, C.SS.R.

30/-

". . . there is no denying that his work as a whole is a masterpiece, a deeply pondered, beautifully constructed doctrinal synthesis, full of the light and sweetness of a noble intelligence entirely dedicated to the noblest of subject matters . . . it is far too powerful a work not to have a profound effect on speculative theology in the Church for many years to come. It is the kind of book that can alter one's whole view of the subject. From one point of view it is a challenge to the scholastic theology of the Catholic manuals, and one that cannot be ignored."

Fr. Kenelm Foster, O.P. in *Blackfriars*

"This is a most impressive and inspiring piece of work by a French theologian. A brief review cannot hope to do justice to it. . . . This beautifully produced and richly suggestive book may be freely commended to all who hold the faith of the Resurrection."

*The British Weekly*

"Anyone who takes an interest in theology, whether priest or layman, specialist or amateur, should find this book exhilarating. The book is quite free from jargon, and indeed both author and translator seem to have avoided many technical expressions which one might have regarded as indispensable. This gives the book a force and directness which no doubt accounts for its powerful impact." *The Catholic Herald*